Personal Magnetism

Personal Magnetism

Discover Your Own Charisma and Learn to Charm, Inspire, and Influence Others

Andrew J. DuBrin

AMACOM
American Management Association
New York • Atlanta • Boston • Chicago • Kansas City • San Francisco • Washington, D.C.
Brussels • Mexico City • Tokyo • Toronto

This book is available at a special discount when ordered in bulk quantities. For information, contact Special Sales Department, AMACOM, a division of American Management Association, 1601 Broadway, New York, NY 10019.

This publication is designed to provide accurate and authoritative information in regard to the subject matter covered. It is sold with the understanding that the publisher is not engaged in rendering legal, accounting, or other professional service. If legal advice or other expert assistance is required, the services of a competent professional person should be sought.

Library of Congress Cataloging-in-Publication Data

DuBrin, Andrew J.
Personal magnetism : discover your own charisma and learn to charm, inspire, and influence others / Andrew J. DuBrin.
p. cm.
Includes bibliographical references and index.
ISBN 0-8144-7936-7 (pbk.)
1. Charisma (Personality trait) I. Title.
BF698.35.C45D83 1997
158.2—dc21 97-11795
CIP

Printing number

10 9 8 7 6 5 4 3 2 1

To
Rosemary and **Clare,**
and their magnetic personalities

Contents

Acknowledgments

My primary thanks on this project go to my editors at AMACOM, Mary Glenn and Richard L. Gatjens. My production editor, Lydia Lewis, also receives my appreciation. Thanks also to my researchers on this project, Claire Denis in Montréal, Québec, and Wanda Perez in Rochester, New York. Both women receive my gratitude for the excitement and hard work they invested in this project. Also receiving credit here are the many magnetic individuals I have encountered and observed in my work and personal life.

Introduction

Why do some people who are not the most talented, best educated, or best looking and who don't come from the most supportive families often accomplish such ends as the following?

- Earn higher incomes
- Get promoted more frequently
- Escape being downsized
- Be chosen for significant leadership positions
- Receive more meaningful task force assignments
- Get elected to office
- Close more sales
- Close bigger sales
- Receive a large share of the company budget
- Launch businesses that become successful
- Have outstanding people in their networks
- Find and hold on to more interesting friends
- More readily find and attract romantic partners
- Have an ample supply of tennis, golfing, or fishing buddies

Several plausible reasons can be identified to explain why some people gain so many advantages. Perhaps they are just lucky; perhaps they have good human relations skills or know how to play politics both on and off the job. Conceivably, they combine all three factors. My research and observations suggest an even deeper reason. A major success factor in work and personal life is the possession of *personal magnetism.* The term refers to a captivating, inspiring personality with charm and charismatic-like qualities. Personal magnetism underlies other success factors such as having good interpersonal skills and powers of persuasion.

Most people think of personal magnetism and its biggest component, charisma, as a mystical quality that a person either has or doesn't have. Following this logic, some people inherit qualities that enable them to become personally magnetic. All others are destined to a life without magnetism. In reality, personal magnetism is like other dimensions of human behavior. Some people have stronger predispositions toward being personally magnetic, and their development of this powerful personality dimension flows naturally. Other people have much less personal magnetism but do not score zero in this regard. In the same way some people are highly intelligent, while others are less intelligent—but virtually nobody has zero intelligence.

A strong note of optimism is that the vast majority of people have the capability to develop an effective and usable degree of magnetism. Research has shown that some components of magnetism and charisma—such as expressing feelings frequently—can be learned.

The purpose of this book is to help serious-minded career people enhance their personal magnetism. If you are hoping to become personally magnetic by learning a handful of habits or inspired thoughts, you will be disappointed. Enhancing your magnetism requires learning a number of skills and attitudes that you can apply to a given situation as needed. For example, in one situation your magnetism might be enhanced by the right type of extraverbal (or nonverbal) communication. In another situation, the appropriate type of flattery will establish your magnetism. Yet in another situation you might need to apply the method of applied psychology known as neurolinguistic programming.

Before previewing the contents of this book, keep in mind that personal magnetism is not a substitute for talent, technical skill, knowledge of the business, creativity, intuition, good work habits, information technology skills, or political skill. Personal magnetism supplements and multiplies the effectiveness of other success factors. The person who combines the skills just mentioned with personal magnetism will most likely achieve career success *and* personal satisfaction.

To enhance your personal magnetism, the information in this book is organized as follows:

Chapter 1 explains in depth the meaning of personal magnetism and its application to gaining the cooperation and support of others as well as its relevance to other worthwhile ends.

Chapter 2 gives you suggestions for finding ways to make insightful interpretations of events and how to translate criticism and negative observations into positive suggestions. You will also learn how to use the speech patterns of charismatic leaders.

Chapter 3 explains how emotional expressiveness is the major ingredient of personal magnetism or charisma. You will also learn how energy and excitement contribute to emotional expressiveness and receive suggestions for responding constructively to the emotions of others.

Chapter 4 gives you current information on how to use extraverbal communication to appear personally magnetic. Among the key aspects of extraverbal communication are your walk, voice tone, and gestures.

Chapter 5 presents practical suggestions for paying people the type of compliments that project an image of personal magnetism. In addition, you will receive suggestions for capitalizing on the power of positive feedback.

Chapter 6 lays the groundwork for improving your standing on key charismatic traits such as humanism, optimism, enthusiasm, and self-confidence. Although I am not promising a personality makeover, most people can modify these traits to their advantage.

Chapter 7 describes a variety of actions and attitudes you can develop that will help you form emotional bonds with others. Among them are using warmth to get others to like you, taking personal risks, and having an energy and action orientation.

Chapter 8 reinforces the idea that humor is an important contributor to personal magnetism and charisma. You will learn about the psychology behind humor, such as looking for the incongruities in situations and switching mental tracks.

Chapter 9 explains how to use neurolinguistic programming to be perceived as magnetic and charming. A basic example is mirroring the posture and breathing patterns of the person you are attempting to influence.

Chapter 10 shows how your work approach can project magnetism. Among such positive work behaviors are love of the task itself, being cool under pressure, and developing a cluster of relevant skills.

This book has a rhythm and a format that you should anticipate. First I introduce a key idea about personal magnetism and then I present an illustrative example or case history. At times public figures will be mentioned to illustrate a point. Suggestions will often be presented in checklist fashion to give you better hooks for learning. At many places you will also have an opportunity to take a self-quiz so that you can rate your current standing on a specific component of personal magnetism.

1

What Personal Magnetism Can Do for You

Some people get noticed, get listened to, get promoted, get funded, and receive help from strangers when lost without even asking. Many others who work equally hard, are equally talented, and have comparable physical appearances struggle to achieve similar outcomes. The difference between these two groups of people usually lies in one having sufficient *personal magnetism* to draw attention to themselves. The term *personal magnetism*, as used here, refers to a captivating, inspiring personality that includes charm and charismatic qualities.

Personal magnetism is a fuzzy concept, but its lack of scientific specificity does not take away from its importance for career and personal life. Many other fuzzy concepts, such as love, loyalty, and leadership, also have a big impact on one's life.

The purpose of this book is to give you the knowledge and tools needed to enhance your personal magnetism. To be mentally set to benefit from the knowledge and tools, it is important for you to take two preliminary steps. First, I want you to think through the signs that your personal magnetism may need bolstering. Second, I want you to understand the powerful benefits that derive from being personally magnetic.

Signs That Your Personal Magnetism Needs Strengthening

Let's assume that you are hardworking and technically competent, make a satisfactory appearance, and have at least average political astuteness. Insufficient personal magnetism could be your problem if you have had several or more of the following experiences:

1. Your career has been on a plateau for a long time in terms of new assignments and/or promotions.
2. You have been a downsizing victim at two or more firms.
3. People rarely ask your opinion during a meeting.
4. You were absent from a meeting and nobody commented later that you were missed.
5. Almost nobody asks you to become a member of his or her network.
6. When assigned to a new team or task force, you are rarely nominated to be the leader.
7. Your jokes and attempts at witty comment rarely receive much of a reaction from others.
8. Co-workers seldom mention your name during meetings or other forums.
9. Statements you make are rarely quoted by co-workers or superiors.
10. You frequently make a statement or volunteer your opinion during a meeting and you barely receive a reaction.
11. A co-worker receives a compliment for wearing a certain suit. Yet when you wore almost the identical suit, nobody complimented you.
12. People who report to you rarely act inspired.
13. People who report to you will go directly to your boss when facing a major problem.
14. The number of times you telephone friends and acquaintances far exceeds the number of times they call you.
15. You rarely receive e-mail messages from friends and acquaintances unless it is in response to your message.
16. While you were attending school, you were almost never nominated to be the captain of a team or club.
17. When between relationships, you have to work extra hard to find a date because others seldom take the initiative to ask you.
18. When in a supermarket, nobody ever turns to you and says, "Here, why don't you go ahead of me. You are probably in more of a rush than I am."

19. Strangers rarely smile at you.
20. When in a public building or airport, a stranger rarely opens the door for you.
21. When at a social gathering of mixed ages, little children seldom talk to you or stand close by you.
22. When at a social gathering, you usually have to initiate conversations because few people start talking to you spontaneously.
23. You receive very few compliments either on or off the job.
24. People tend to yawn frequently in face-to-face interactions with you.
25. You cannot recall anyone ever saying that you are dynamic or that you have a sparkling personality.

Very few people would be able to say that they have had none or only one of these experiences. Yet having many of the twenty-five experiences is a strong indication that your level of personal magnetism is low enough to be blocking potential happiness in your work and personal life. Assiduously applying the ideas offered throughout this book will most likely elevate your level of personal magnetism. For now, let's dig further into some of the ways in which personal magnetism will lead to positive outcomes in your life.

Strengthening and Embellishing Your Relationships With Others

For many people the biggest payoff from having a high standing on personal magnetism is that it leads to closer, warmer relationships with others. If you are personally magnetic, others are eager to enter into business and social relationships with you. A key contributing factor is that many people find it rewarding to associate with a person they perceive to be personally magnetic.

As with charisma, a key term in understanding personal magnetism is *perception*. Magnetism is an interpretation of your characteristics by another person. If you implement every suggestion for becoming personally magnetic, you will still not capture everybody. To be personally magnetic means that a large percentage of the people with whom you interact will perceive you as charming and scintillating. To be personally magnetic, however, does not mean that 100 percent of the people with whom you interact will be strongly attracted by your presence. A sensible goal in increasing your personal magnetism is therefore to increase the probability that a given individual will find you appealing for work or social purposes.

A friend of mine, Kenneth Rabinowitz, is a successful consultant in interpersonal skills and customer service training. He heads a large firm that continues to expand and prosper even during the downside of business activity. He also teaches in an executive development program at a university. Ken receives outstanding evaluations from the managers who take his course.

Curious as to the reasons for Ken's success with clients, I asked him what accounted for his impressive following. Ken really didn't have a good answer. He alluded to the fact that his firm had high-quality training programs, a competent staff, and more than its share of good luck. Thinking that perhaps Ken was too modest to explain the reasons for his success, I spoke to two people who had attended his training programs. (I met these people in another context, and both volunteered the information that they had been to one of Ken's training programs.)

Carol, a customer service supervisor, explained what she liked about the program she attended. "The man is so likable, so dynamic, it makes learning enjoyable," she said. "I was familiar with some of the information in his program. But the way he delivered the material was so interesting, his ideas really hit home."

Steve, a technical support manager, offered praise with a similar theme. He said, "Ken Rabinowitz really delivered. He made some material that could have been dry come alive. The guy really adds value. He believes so strongly in what he is doing that he converts you."

The message is that Ken the trainer draws praise from clients partially on the basis of the content of his programs, but to an even greater degree from the relationship he forms with them. Ken has a magnetic appeal that leads people attending his seminars to praise him and the program. Positive word of mouth leads to more clients, which in turn leads to more positive word of mouth, and the success cycle continues.

Personal magnetism also builds strong relationships in personal life. Betty McIntyre, age 73, recently retired from a successful career as a fund raiser. My primary concern here, however, is Betty's success in personal life. Betty married her fourth husband three years ago. Before you conclude that Betty runs into conflict with men, keep in mind that Betty is a three-time widow. Attracting a husband at age 70 is notable because unattached women in her age bracket outnumber unattached men by a ratio of six to one.

Betty attracts men not on the basis of her looks, though she is attractive and well-groomed, but so are many of her age mates who are not even able to find dates. Betty has done well in her career, so you may think that it is her pension that attracted her last two husbands. Strike out that potential explanation. Betty's new husband has a net worth exceeding hers by a factor of five.

In interviewing Betty and observing her reactions, the reasons she attracts life partners becomes apparent. Betty has a warmth and playfulness about her that many men would find comforting. She smiles frequently, and makes reassuring gestures with her eyes, face, and hands. She speaks in a low tone that soothes and reassures. Her presence projects emotional support, understanding, and strength. Perhaps the same qualities that attract men to Betty also attracted fund donors during her career.

Ken and Betty are but two examples of how being personally magnetic leads to improved personal relationships. The deeper issue is *why* being personally magnetic gives a person an edge in interpersonal relationships. What's in it for the people who are being magnetized? Awareness of these factors can sometimes help shape your appeal to others. The benefits people derive from associating with an individual they perceive to be personally magnetic and charismatic include the following:

- *People will gravitate toward someone they perceive to be a winner because they like to bask in that person's glory.* The winner factor enters the picture because magnetic people are often perceived as winners. To complicate the issue, winners are often perceived to be personally magnetic.

- *People are attracted to a magnetic person because the latter arouses a positive emotional response in them.* The emotional response is similar physiologically to sexual attraction or to the reaction you might have to a glorious painting, photograph, poem, or automobile. If the person attracted to you in the first place receives the anticipated emotional response, he or she will be back for more.

• *People are attracted to someone they perceive as personally charismatic because they feel that the association will bolster their self-esteem.* It works this way: If one person is attracted to and forms a positive relationship with another (the personally magnetic one), it means that he or she has been accepted by somebody important. And acceptance by somebody important is a major contributor to self-esteem.

• *People seek out others they perceive to be personally magnetic because of a desire for affection inside or outside of the workplace.* Affection enters the picture because to be liked by somebody warm and charming is a potent driver of affection.

• *Similarly, people seek out others who are personally magnetic because to capture their attention is a potent form of recognition.* Have you ever noticed how wealthy people fawn over athletes? Or how they proudly display photographs of themselves with athletes or other public figures? Association with a charismatic person gives many people the recognition they crave. The recognition accrues even if the magnetic person is not famous.

• *Many people want to work for or with a personally magnetic individual because it energizes and motivates them.* To these people it is exciting to work closely with an appealing person. Personally magnetic individuals and the organization alike benefit from the motivational surge experienced by those who want to associate with a person they consider to be highly appealing.

Influencing Others in the Direction You Choose

The most compelling advantage of personal magnetism and charisma is that they enhance one's ability to influence others. People are much more likely to follow a course of action you recommend when they perceive you to be personally magnetic. Many people have said about a charismatic executive, "I would gamble my career to work for him." Gambling a career in these instances often means that the person will leave a relatively secure job to join the executive in a start-up venture.

Ron Brown, the late U.S. secretary of commerce, represents a good model of how personal magnetism can facilitate exerting influence. Brown was perceived by his admirers and critics alike as exuding natural charm. His charm helped him transform the Department of Commerce into an effective vehicle for promoting U.S. exports. Foreign officials enjoyed doing business with Brown, and he was regarded as a superior bridge builder.[1]

The contribution of personal magnetism to influencing others can be better understood by examining how magnetism enhances several specific influence tactics.

Leading by Example

A simple but effective way of influencing others is to lead by example. You lead, or influence, others by serving as a positive role model. One area in which a manager might lead by example would be to communicate certain aspects of the organizational culture. You, as a leader, can communicate values and expectations by your own actions. Particularly well suited to leading by example are actions showing loyalty, self-sacrifice, and service beyond the call of duty. During crunch time on a project, you might work sixty-five hours per week to demonstrate the value of self-sacrifice that is included in the culture.

The rub is that people are much more likely to use you as a role model if, for them, you have a magnetic appeal. So despite the popularity of leading by example, it may not work well unless the person setting the example is appealing to the people who are supposed to follow him or her as a model.

Rational Persuasion

The traditional way of influencing people through rational persuasion is still an important tactic. Rational persuasion involves using logical arguments and factual evidence to convince another person that a proposal or request is workable and is likely to achieve a goal.

In general, assertiveness combined with careful research are necessary to make rational persuasion an effective tactic. It is likely to be most effective with people who are intelligent and rational. Yet even intelligent and rational people engage in selective perception. They are more likely to listen to the hard evidence contained in an argument when the person delivering the message is warm and likable. Personal magnetism makes logic appear even more logical.

Exchanging Favors

Offering to exchange favors if another person will help you accomplish a task is another standard influence tactic. By making an exchange you strike a bargain with the other party. The exchange often translates into being willing to reciprocate at a later date. The exchange might also involve promising a share of the benefits if the other person helps you accomplish a task. For example, you might promise to place a person's name on a report to top management if that person helps analyze the data and prepare the tables.

Another perspective on exchange is that you are building a favor bank. In other words, you do favors for people today with the expectation that you can make a withdrawal from the favor bank. A human resources manager took the initiative to help a colleague in another company recruit a physically disabled compensation analyst. Several months later the same human resources manager called on the colleague to nominate her for office in their professional society.

Exchange works more effectively when the person initiating the deal is personally magnetic. The nature of the exchange (such as "If you work extra hours now, you can have compensatory time off in the future") should have perceived value to the recipient. Nevertheless, if the person making the offer is personally magnetic, the proposition is more likely to be accepted. A dealer was asked by a sales manager to load up on a difficult-to-sell item (a washer-dryer combination). In exchange, the dealer would receive an ample supply of next year's fastest-selling item. The dealer commented about the exchange, "If I didn't think so much of Pete [the sales manager] as a person, I would never have considered the deal."

Developing a Network of Resource Persons

Networking is an important strategy for career management, including becoming an influential person. The ability to establish a network and call on support when it is needed helps a manager or professional exert influence. A branch bank manager used his network of resource persons when he needed additional space for his operation. His direct influence target was his immediate superior, but he also had to influence members of his network. He describes how he achieved his goal:

> My strategy was to convince my immediate superior that the current facilities were too small to not only manage the current volume of business, but too small to allow us to increase our market share in a rapidly growing area. First, I persuaded my manager to visit the branch more often, especially when the branch was very busy. I also solicited my accountant's help to provide statistical reports on a regular basis that communicated the amount of overall growth in the area, as well as the growth of my competitors. These reports showed that our market share had increased.
>
> I then asked my superior to visit with me as I called on several prospects in the area. This would let him know the types of potential business in the area. During this time I kept pushing to increase all levels of business at the branch.
>
> Finally, I encouraged key bank customers to say favorable things about my branch when they visited with my senior managers. Eventually my boss got behind my proposal. We were able to build an addition to the building which allowed me to add several new employees.[2]

Among the major players in the bank manager's network were his key customers. With the prevailing attitude that the customer is king or queen, the customers' favorable comments made the manager's manager more receptive to the former's proposition. A contributing factor to the customers' willingness to help the branch manager was his magnetic personality. The customers enjoyed doing business with him and experienced personal satisfaction in helping him with his ploy.

Forming Coalitions

At times it is difficult to influence an individual or group by acting alone. A manager will then have to form coalitions, or alliances, with others to create the necessary clout. Coalition formation works as an influence tactic because, to quote an old adage, "there is power in numbers." Coalitions in business and government are a numbers game—the more people you can get on your side, the better. The more powerful the manager, the less need there is for forming a coalition. Yet there are times when even a powerful manager needs to multiply his or her power to accomplish a major goal.

In forming coalitions, as with other influence tactics, a key underlying factor is personal magnetism. It is the fuel that gives the influence tactic its extra power. People are much more likely to join your coalition if you inspire them with your personal magnetism and charisma.

Building Your Power Base

Closely related to the advantage of having personal magnetism for influencing others is building a power base. Having power makes it easier for a person to exercise influence. How a person builds a power base is as broad as the subject of organizational politics. The reason is that the purpose of politics is to acquire power. My specific concern here is to explain how personal magnetism contributes to acquiring power. The general point is that by being personally magnetic, along with having other assets, a person acquires power. And even when you rely on other techniques—such as knowing the right people—to acquire power, magnetism helps you implement those techniques.

A 1996 *Fortune* magazine article describes Jill Barad as being one of the most powerful women executives in the United States, having become CEO of toy maker Mattel in 1996. In addition to her overall managerial and leadership skills and good market sense, Barad flaunts her magnetism. She greets key business associates with hugs and kisses and dresses in a flamboyantly feminine fashion.[3] Barad's brand of magnetism has helped her rise from her starting position as a product manager at Mattel in 1981 to the top of the ladder fifteen years later.

Next we look at two specific methods—the use of expertise and the use of one's prestige—for developing one's power base and at how personal magnetism supports and facilitates using each particular method. Without magnetism, many methods of acquiring power may fall flat.

Expert Power

A person who has talent, skill, and knowledge can acquire and exercise power. Expert power is the ability to influence others through specialized knowledge, skill, or abilities, as does the marketing manager who is adept at opening up new markets. The vast majority of people who have become powerful launched their careers by exercising expert power. Jill Barad garnered power for herself by dramatically expanding the appeal of the Barbie doll. (Whether or not the Barbie doll is good for the self-image of little girls, Barbie's success helped put Barad in orbit.)

A recommended method of acquiring expert power is to become a subject matter expert in the area that fits the present or future needs of the firm. Current examples include knowing how to establish attractive Web sites for the firm or open markets in China. Even if you are a subject matter expert, being personally magnetic contributes to cashing in on your expertise. If you are personally magnetic, people in positions of authority are more likely to give you a good opportunity to display your expertise. You have probably heard somebody lament, "I could have accomplished the same thing as ______ if they had just given me a chance." The other person may well have been given the chance because of his or her warmth and sparkle.

Prestige Power

Prestige power stems from a person's status and reputation. A manager who has accumulated important business success acquires prestige power. Executive recruiters (headhunters) are eager to keep on file the names of managers with prestige power. Prestige power, of course, takes a long time to develop. It is a desirable state to work toward. Prestige power requires more personal magnetism to acquire than does expert power. Being personally magnetic bolsters your image in such a way that your visibility increases.

Larry Bossidy, the CEO of AlliedSignal, is a prime example of the combination of prestige power and personal magnetism. His reputation is so positive that he has been labeled the most sought-after executive in America. Several years ago, Bossidy was courted for the top position at IBM (before Louis Gerstner arrived). He has an imposing physical presence and is imbued with dozens of other leadership characteristics.

A manager who worked at GE while Bossidy was the number-two executive in the company, said: "Bossidy had an enormous following at GE. He set such clear visions for us that we all knew where we were headed. As tough as Bossidy is, we knew he had a heart of gold. He was like the firm, lovable uncle most people would want in their family."

Enhancing Your Self-Esteem and Self-Confidence

A vital, positive consequence of being personally magnetic is that it usually bolsters a person's self-esteem and self-confidence. To accept this conclusion, you must first accept a bit of circular logic. Being personally magnetic may bolster your self-esteem and self-confidence, whereas the reverse is also true to some extent. High self-esteem and self-confidence contribute to personal magnetism.

First, let's look at the self-esteem building aspects of personal magnetism. People who are personally magnetic behave and think in many of the ways associated with self-esteem, including the following:

- They are excited about starting each day.
- When handed a challenging assignment they dive in with confidence.
- They speak up, set limits, and say no without anxiety.

- They don't make excuses for their mistakes.
- They are able to shrug off minor mistakes.
- Someone else's bad mood doesn't affect their good mood.
- They don't care how much money someone else makes.
- They think for themselves.
- Hard work exhilarates them.[4]

The personally magnetic individual is therefore likely to behave and think in a manner that bolsters self-esteem. It is also true that people who develop personal magnetism will experience more self-esteem. Yet the reverse is not necessarily true. Many people with high self-esteem rate low on personal magnetism despite their other good qualities. For example, many physical scientists who are proud of what they do and feel good about themselves, yet are quiet and reserved, have high self-esteem.

Personal magnetism contributes to self-confidence in several important ways. The most general way in which personal magnetism builds self-confidence is that magnetic individuals have so many positive experiences; so many doors are opened for them on and off the job. If people take you more seriously, nominate you for good positions, and seek out your friendship, your self-confidence automatically grows.

A major self-confidence builder is that others gravitate toward the magnetic person, often paying compliments and smiling. As a result of these smiles and compliments, the personally magnetic individual experiences a frequent self-confidence booster.

A specific way in which personal magnetism boosts self-confidence is that the magnetic person is physically touched by so many others. Being touched by others is a natural self-confidence builder, particularly when the touching signifies acceptance and adulation.

Visualize for a moment a time when you heard and watched a dynamic speaker. After the speech was completed, many people probably walked up to the speaker and shook his or her hand, or tapped the speaker's arm. Later on, as participants left the conference room, more congratulatory touching probably took place. Personally magnetic people will experience this same type of touching in both work and social settings apart from speech making.

The touching just referred to is not necessarily sexually oriented. Yet personally magnetic people probably experience less uninvited sexual touching than others do. A possible reason is that the dignity projected by magnetic people may deter some would-be offenders from this practice. Sexual harassers tend to make advances toward people they perceive as having less power and status than themselves—at least in a business office. A new form of sexual harassment emerging in a medical setting is that some male patients sexually harass their women physicians, although in this situation, it is the lower-status person who harasses the higher-status person.

Bringing Joy and Solace to Others

Personally magnetic people frequently donate their time and money toward directly assisting others. Magnetic individuals benefit simultaneously because they experience the joy of helping others. A case in point is Deeprak Chopra, the self-help guru with millions of loyal followers. He is known for the emotional link he forms with his readers and listeners. According to "The Law of Giving" he espouses, the more we give, the more we'll receive. Chopra offers the following anecdote in support of the law:

> I had parked in a dark, deserted lot. A young kid approached me—at most 10 years old—and said, "Sir, I have a baby sister, and I need some money." Something about the way he said this was so sweet. I looked in my wallet, took out a $20 bill and gave it to him. You should have seen his eyes! He said, "Thank you sir. God bless you."
>
> Then he looked at me again and asked, "Are you Dr. Chopra? Are you practicing The Law of Giving?" This is an absolutely true story. The result? I felt so good giving him $20. I only wished I had given him more. And the rest of the week has been bliss because I keep thinking of this kid and the joy I got.[5]

Enhancing Your Leadership Effectiveness

A major work-related benefit from being personally magnetic is that it helps you to be a more effective leader. Being personally magnetic increases the chances that you will be nominated for a leadership position and that you will be effective in this capacity. Personal magnetism is closely linked to charisma, a topic that receives separate attention in Chapter 6.

Personal magnetism contributes substantially to leadership effectiveness, but it works best in combination with less glamorous skills such as planning and organizing. A germane example is Marco Landi, the head of Apple Europe. Landi is a popular and charismatic leader, but he is also a rigorous manager. When he took charge of Apple Europe, he imposed discipline and accountability on the free-wheeling computer maker. For instance, he achieved a 20 percent reduction in costs by jettisoning country-by-country marketing. In its place, he reorganized the management lines around markets and business processes such as sales, marketing, and distribution.[6]

The general contribution of personal magnetism to leadership effectiveness is that being magnetic helps a person carry out the key aspects of a leader's role: persuading, inspiring, influencing, motivating others, and getting them to buy into your vision. The influencing aspects of personal magnetism have already been described. Other aspects of magnetism that contribute to leadership effectiveness, such as being emotionally expressive and having charismatic traits, are described throughout the rest of this book.

You will gain another perspective on how personal magnetism contributes to leadership by examining leadership roles or expectations. Successfully carrying out several of these roles is facilitated by personal magnetism.

• *Figurehead.* Leaders, particularly high-ranking managers, spend some of their time engaging in ceremonial activities or acting as figureheads. Four specific behaviors fit the figurehead role of a leader:

1. Entertaining clients or customers as an official representative of the organization
2. Making oneself available to outsiders as a representative of the organization
3. Serving as an official representative of the organization at gatherings outside the organization
4. Escorting official visitors

You might think that this type of work could easily be done by the comely store associate who sprays perfume on willing customers. Yet in reality, being magnetic makes you a more effective figurehead. Effective leaders generate enthusiasm even while flipping hamburgers and grilling chicken at a company picnic. Imbued with a winning personality, the magnetic leader is an effective figurehead because he or she sells outsiders on the virtues of the organization.

- *Spokesperson.* When a leader acts as a spokesperson, the emphasis is on answering letters, e-mail messages, or inquiries and on formally reporting to individuals and groups directly outside the leader's organizational unit. As a spokesperson, the managerial leader keeps five groups of people informed about the unit's activities, plans, capabilities, and vision. The five groups are (1) upper-level management, (2) customers or clients, (3) other important outsiders such as labor unions, (4) professional colleagues, and (5) the general public.

A leader does not need personal magnetism merely to send messages about the group's activities to outsiders. Yet a message powered by personal magnetism is more likely to be listened to and believed. Magnetism helps messages get through in an environment in which multiple messages are competing for attention.

- *Negotiator.* Part of almost any manager's job is trying to make deals with others for needed resources. Three specific negotiating activities are: (1) bargaining with superiors for funds, facilities, equipment, or other forms of support; (2) bargaining with other units in the organization for the use of staff, facilities, equipment, or other forms of support; and (3) bargaining with suppliers and vendors for services, schedules, and delivery times.

Leaders and managers vary considerably in their negotiation skills. The most effective negotiators use standard negotiating tactics such as granting small concessions along the way. In addition, they have the flair and sense of drama that requires personal magnetism.

During a negotiation between representatives of a consumer electronics company and one of its small suppliers, the supplier's company president said: "With all my heart I would like to meet your price. But if I do it means laying off three of my best workers.

What would you do if you were in my place?'' At this point, negotiations turned in the president's favor. He received a price for the components that he thought was equitable and that enabled him to avoid a layoff.

• *Coach.* An effective leader takes time to coach team members. Specific behaviors in the role include (1) recognizing team members' achievements; (2) providing team members with feedback concerning ineffective performance; and (3) ensuring that team members are informed of steps that can improve their performance.

A leader can function adequately as a coach by going through the mechanics of coaching such as listening and providing feedback. Most outstanding coaches in the workplace or on the athletic field, however, are magnetic personalities who inspire team members during face-to-face interactions.

• *Team Builder.* A key aspect of a leader's role is to build an effective team. Activities contributing to this role include (1) ensuring that team members are recognized for their accomplishments, such as through memos of appreciation; (2) initiating activities that contribute to group morale, such as giving parties and sponsoring sports teams; and (3) holding periodic staff meetings to encourage team members to talk about their accomplishments, problems, and concerns.

As with the four other leadership roles mentioned here, personal magnetism enhances being a team builder. The presence of a magnetic and charismatic leader helps unify and focus the group's activity, resulting in enhanced teamwork.

Our journey toward enhanced personal magnetism has begun. We have looked at the signs suggesting that your level of personal magnetism might need strenghtening. We have described six key benefits of being personally magnetic:

1. Strengthening and embellishing your relationships with others
2. Influencing others in the direction you choose
3. Building your power base
4. Enhancing your self-esteem and self-confidence

5. Bringing joy and solace to others
6. Enhancing your leadership effectiveness

The stage has now been set for developing the understanding, insight, and skills you need to elevate your level of personal magnetism. The balance of the book deals with sensible, specific ways of developing personal magnetism. The intention is to make the abstract and mystical concept of personal magnetism more concrete and down-to-earth.

2

Projecting Magnetism Through Language and Thinking Patterns

Speaking and thinking like a personally magnetic individual is one of the most effective ways to be perceived by others as having personal magnetism. By practicing the mental habits that come so naturally to charismatic individuals you can substantially enhance the impact you have on others.

Learning about the language and thinking patterns of personally magnetic individuals will help you appreciate that magnetism is not simply a superficial quality such as smiling frequently and remembering people's names. People with magnetism attract others to their way of thinking in large part because of the mental stimulation they offer. Magnetic people offer a pleasant change of pace from mundane thinking, bland language, and the ordinary interpretation of events.

Use Colorful Expressions and Slogans

Scott McNealy, the chief executive of Sun Microsystems Inc., is a passionate and inspiring leader who is one of Silicon Valley's most respected managers. Staffers at Sun are energized by his speech. When assessing a rival product, Microsoft's Window and MS-DOS, he described it as "whip cream on a road apple." He described part of his philosophy of doing business as "kick butt and have fun."[1]

The point illustrated by McNealy's colorful expressions is that personally magnetic people enliven their speech with offbeat, colorful, memorable language. Typically they make up their own expressions, or use those not suffering from overexposure. (Magnetic people, for example, are less likely to say, "This isn't rocket science" or "You can't make an omelette without breaking an egg.")

Use Forceful and Powerful Expressions

Certain words used in the proper context give power and force to speech, thus enhancing magnetism. Used comfortably, naturally, and sincerely, these words help influence and inspire others. Current buzzwords usually have a heavy impact. Note the emphasis on *current*. Yesterday's buzzwords have low impact. Presented next is a sampling of powerful and forceful expressions:

- Tell group members that you want them to *unleash their creative potential* instead of simply asking them to make a few suggestions.
- Talk about being *at the center of a revolution* instead of quietly incorporating an important new work method.
- Use the term *on the verge of accomplishing something* so long as a project is in process.
- Mention that you want employees to *bond* with customers instead of simply stating that you want them to establish a good working relationship.
- If you have taken into account a customer requirement in offering a new service or product, say that what you are offering is *customer-driven.*
- If you think your company should profit more from its mistakes, say that the firm should become a *learning organization.*
- Ask the group to *do it right the first time* instead of just asking them to avoid mistakes.
- When your department has won an interdepartmental skirmish, or won a bid over a competitor, mention that you have *nuked*

them. "Nuking" is more powerful than simply winning (except when used in reference to a microwave oven).

Inspire Others With Metaphors and Analogies

A well-chosen analogy or metaphor can appeal to the intellect, the imagination, and the values of those hearing it. An analogy draws attention to the similarity between the features of two things, so people can make a comparison. On and off the job, people are excited and inspired by analogies relevant to the challenges they face. Here is a sampling of analogies leaders have used in their interactions with group members:

> "We are a young company competing against the established giants, much like Compaq Computer of fifteen years ago."
>
> "Our clients must trust us with their money, just as they trust their family internist to do what is in their best interest."
>
> "As financial planners we provide a service to our clients as important as the help they receive from their accountants and lawyers."
>
> "Just like the bottom-seeded team that made it to the final four of the NCAA basketball tournament, we are the sentimental favorite to win this contract."
>
> "As information systems experts, our contribution to the company is similar to the role played by the nervous system in the human body."

A metaphor is also a comparison, but the comparison is between two objects not ordinarily associated with each other. For example, a human resources manager might state, "Don't be concerned that many people have a very limited understanding of what we do for the organization. Think of the situation of a tree. Many people just see what is on the surface, and have a limited appreciation of its function. What they do not realize is that the tree moderates the temperature in the adjacent building, and helps prevent floods. We also make an enormous contribution that can go unnoticed."

The manager of a firm that offers an advisory service, such as crisis management, might say to the group, "Our department is like four-wheel drive. We are ever vigilant, waiting to be called into action to get somebody through a difficult situation."

Offer Penetrating Insights

A distinguishing intellectual strength of magnetic individuals is that they are able to size up situations and people and arrive at an in-depth understanding that others might miss. Penetrating insights are magnetic because they offer people assistance in spotting trends and interpreting events that they might not see for themselves. A penetrating insight thus goes beyond the obvious. (The term *penetrating insight* is redundant, because an insight penetrates. Note that *pénétration* is the French word for "insight.")

A major advantage of an insight is that it helps another person to understand a situation more clearly, including the illogic in his or her own thinking. The other person will often be appreciative of your efforts and be drawn to you because of your contribution.

A Few Magnetic Insights

Let's begin with an example of insight into another person's behavior that surfaces in several forms. It is especially useful in helping people to overcome rationalizations and procrastination.

Melinda is 38 years old and works as an office supervisor. She is contemplating attending a two-year college at night because she fears if she does not attain an associate's degree her job security will be in jeopardy. Melinda says to a friend, "I know I should go back to school. But I figure it will take four years for me to earn an associate's degree. I'll be 42 by then. That's almost old enough to be a grandmother."

Melinda's friend replies, "How old will you be in four years if you don't get your degree?"

Melinda at first laughs. She then suddenly realizes that time will pass by whether or not she fills it with an important personal and professional accomplishment. Melinda now recognizes that worrying about how old she will be when she receives her degree is self-defeating behavior.

Andrew Grove, CEO of Intel, the computer chip manufacturer, has been a well-known business leader for many years. His photograph frequently appears in business magazines, and his two books on management are widely read. Grove has an affinity for offering provocative insights about business. His favorite motto (insight) is "Only the paranoid survive."

Upon first hearing this statement, people might think that Grove is paranoid. When they think through his motto, however, they realize that in a highly competitive industry like computer chips, suspiciousness and looking over one's shoulder are necessary for success. For example, Grove has spent millions of dollars in legal fees to sue companies for alleged copyright and patent violations.

Another justification for Andrew Grove's suspiciousness is his experience with Japanese chip makers in the mid-1980s. The Japanese manufacturers drove prices so low that they virtually eliminated their U.S. competitors in the market for DRAM memory chips. Grove was particularly irate because Intel had developed the technology for these chips. His business judgment told him to jettison the DRAM chip business and refocus the company in other directions.[2]

Achieving Insights From Feedback

Another way of achieving the type of insights that contribute to magnetism is to interpret feedback deeply. While others might superficially accept feedback, the magnetic person is likely to wring much more meaning out of it.

Consider Phyllis, who has lost three key group members over a six-month time span. She defensively dismissed the problem by saying, "I guess we just don't pay enough to keep good people." Although her initial analysis might be correct, with a well-disciplined self-awareness orientation she could have dug deeper for the reasons behind the turnover. She might have asked, "Is there something in my leadership approach that creates turnover problems?" Or she might have requested the results of her staff's exit interviews, because these sometimes provide valuable information. People leaving the company are more likely to be candid about their work experience than those who are still employed.

Noted organizational psychologist Chris Argyris has coined

the terms *single-loop learning* and *double-loop learning* to differentiate between levels of self-awareness (see Figure 2-1). Single-loop learning is an easy, superficial approach in which learners seek only minimum feedback on problems that if examined honestly and in-depth might force them to confront their basic ideas or ways of acting.[3] Like Phyllis, the single-loop learner thinks defensively, rather like—in the analogy Argyris offers—the thermostat that automatically turns on the heat whenever the room temperature drops below 68 degrees Fahrenheit (20 degrees Celsius).

Double-loop learning requires intense mental concentration. It is an in-depth type of learning that uses feedback to confront the validity of one's thinking in a given situation. For instance, a business owner who has just been cut from a supplier list might say to himself, "Just rotten luck, I guess. The company decided to cut costs so chose a lower-cost, lower-quality supplier." Another business owner included in the supplier cutback might say, "Why were we eliminated as a supplier? I'm angry and disappointed that the

Figure 2-1. Single-loop learning versus double-loop learning.

customer thinks we are less valuable than other suppliers. I'm going to investigate why we were not considered valuable enough to retain."

Double-loop learning contributes to magnetism when the person processing the feedback at a deep level shares these insights gained with the group or with another person. Since most people are not accustomed to such nondefensive, insightful thinking, they will be intellectually stimulated.

To achieve double-loop learning you must minimize any tendencies to defensive thinking. A double-loop learning thermostat would ask, "Why am I set at 68 degrees?" and then ask whether another temperature might more economically achieve the goal of heating the room. Self-awareness and double-loop learning require considerable mental discipline. You have to concentrate carefully on the meaning of feedback. When the feedback could possibly be interpreted in more than one way, say to yourself, "My goal is to gain the edge in as many situations as possible. What message can I squeeze out of this situation? What is the environment telling me?" Then share your insights with those affected by the situation.

Becoming Better at Achieving Insights

Even if you are convinced by now that making insightful interpretations of events will contribute to your magnetism, there is plenty of hard work ahead. Enhancing your insights is a form of mental discipline that requires concentrated listening and frequent practice. Keep in mind that the opposite of being insightful is letting messages from others go right over your head. The following suggestions will help you sharpen your insights:

1. When you receive feedback, ask yourself, "Does this have implications for my usual modus operandi?"
2. When observing general news events or those related to business, ask yourself, "What is the implication of this information for my job?"
3. When you receive an ambiguous message from someone in the organization, ask yourself, "What is this person really telling me?"

4. When anything goes wrong at work or at home, ask yourself, "Is this a random event, or is it a wake-up call?" (Assume that you lose your keys. Ponder whether this is something that will probably never happen again or whether it means that you need a fixed place to park your keys?)

5. When engaged in a business activity or pastime, ask yourself, "What are the key factors that make for success in this activity?" (For example, an indoor athletic and tennis club needs to find a way to attract beginners who can attend during the day, such as full-time homemakers and retirees.)

6. After having a stunning insight, remember to share it with others as a vehicle for enhancing your magnetism.

Express Innovative Thoughts

The same kind of mental toughness that enables magnetic people to make penetrating insights contributes to innovativeness. The word *innovative* refers to original, close-to-original, imaginative, or nonstereotypical ideas that can very likely be put into practice. To be innovative is to be creative. Before reading further, take the accompanying self-quiz to think through your current level of innovative thinking.

The Imagination Checklist

Indicate whether you tend to agree or disagree with each of the following statements.

	Agree	Disagree
1. I have won at least one suggestion award in my life.	_______	_______
2. My choice is to give children well-known names such as Bob, Mike, Lisa, and Jennifer.	_______	_______
3. I have entered at least one contest that required the contestants to name a product, name a mascot, or develop a slogan.	_______	_______

4. I am seriously involved in a hobby such as photography, art, or woodworking.	_______	_______
5. Virtually all the photographs I take are of family members or friends.	_______	_______
6. I almost never make up my own greeting cards but instead rely on those prepared professionally.	_______	_______
7. Several times in my life, friends of mine have referred to me as creative.	_______	_______
8. When involved in a group effort, I usually go along with the thinking of the team.	_______	_______
9. I have published or patented something in my life (if only a letter to the editor or an article in my school newspaper).	_______	_______
10. When faced with a problem, I typically accept the first alternative solution that comes to mind.	_______	_______
11. I make frequent use of such expressions as "You can choose your friends but you can't choose your family," and "You don't have to be a rocket scientist to. . . ."	_______	_______
12. Each year I take the same kind of vacation.	_______	_______
13. There are only about four different foods I order when dining out.	_______	_______
14. At least one person I have worked for has said that I was creative.	_______	_______
15. I frequently make comments on the job or in school that cause others to laugh.	_______	_______

Scoring and Interpretation: Give yourself a 1 for *agreeing* with questions 1, 3, 4, 7, 9, 14, and 15. Give yourself a 1 for *disagreeing* with questions 2, 5, 6, 8, 10, 11, 12, and 13. A score of 12 or higher indicates that you probably have good imagination. A score of 11 or lower suggests that you need to think more imaginatively in order to enhance your personal magnetism.

Next we look at two key strategies for developing the type of innovative thinking that will enhance your magnetism: (1) overcoming traditional thinking and (2) using everyday techniques for improving your level of creativity. The strategies are related because everyday techniques for enhancing creativity help you to overcome traditional thinking.

Overcoming Traditional Thinking

The major task in becoming innovative is to learn how to think in nontraditional ways. You must learn to question the status quo even if you can't come up with good alternatives. The start of the cellular telephone revolution began when a manager asked, ''Why can't we find a way to commercialize wireless communication devices like walkie-talkies and CB radios on a much broader scale?'' Technical personnel were then dispatched to find an answer to this question. The revolution in organization structure began when executives and researchers asked, ''Why do we place so much emphasis on hierarchy? Isn't there another way to manage an organization?'' The answer was to rely more on projects and teams, and less on vertical structures.

To make a contribution, and to enhance your magnetism, you don't have to start a new industry or overhaul an organization. Innovation is also important for improving work processes and enhancing customer satisfaction. You can exercise your imagination by investigating how to reduce waste and redundancy in your daily work. This type of investigation is the essence of business process reengineering and work streamlining. Ask, and find answers to, such questions as:

- ''Why does it takes us five days to get an estimate to a customer?''
- ''Why does it take us six days to get a contract to a supplier?''
- ''What can we do about spending two hours per day answering each other's e-mail messages?''
- ''What steps can we take to appear like a bigger, more substantial company to customers and potential customers?''

The person who poses such questions and also proposes good solutions will become known as a fixer, thus contributing to his or her magnetism. Asking the right questions makes a contribution, but the combination of asking questions and providing solutions is obviously more powerful.

The central idea of overcoming traditional thinking has been expressed in several ways, meaning essentially the same thing. Yet looking at several of these perspectives can help jog one's mind into becoming a more innovative thinker:

• *A creative person thinks outside the box.* A box in this sense is a category that confines and restricts thinking. The success of the Starbucks coffeehouses was based on the founder's vision to think outside the box that a coffeehouse must be a locally owned, independent operation.

• *People who are not creative suffer from "hardening of the categories."* A noncreative person thinks categorically, literally placing people and things in categories. In recent years several furniture stores have expanded their market by thinking less categorically about who constitutes a *couple.* Previously, conventional wisdom held that only opposite-sex couples should appear in advertisements about purchasing furniture. Overcoming traditional thinking in this instance translated into developing advertisements that portrayed same-sex couples shopping for furniture together.

• *Creative people engage in lateral thinking in addition to vertical thinking.* Vertical thinking is an analytical, logical process that results in few answers to a problem. The vertical, or critical, thinker is looking for the one best solution to a problem, much like estimating return on assets. In contrast, lateral thinking spreads out to find many different solutions to a problem.

The vertical-thinking manager attempts to find the best possible return on investment in financial terms only. The lateral- or innovative-thinking manager might say, "A financial return on investment is desirable. But let's not restrict our thinking. Customer loyalty, quality, being a good corporate citizen, and satisfied employees are also important returns on investment." (Notice the magnetism displayed by the lateral-thinking manager.)

Ten Everyday Creativity-Building Suggestions

In honing innovative-thinking ability, almost anybody could profit from the suggestions described next. The more of these everyday activities you implement, the more intellectually stimulating you will become. This is important because providing intellectual stimulation to others contributes heavily to personal magnetism.

1. *Keep track of your original ideas by maintaining an idea notebook or computer file.* Few people have such uncluttered minds that they can recall all their past flashes of insight when they need them.

2. *Stay current in your field.* Having current facts at hand gives you the raw material to link information creatively. (In practice, creativity usually takes the form of associating ideas that have previously been unassociated, such as the idea of selling movie tickets with the idea of selling them through vending machines.)

3. *Try to overcome approaches to problems that lock you into one way of doing things.* Avoid becoming a prisoner of familiarity, someone who cannot think about doing things in more than one way.

4. *Participate in creative hobbies.* Do puzzles and exercises or pursue arts and crafts. Learning a second language well also fosters innovation because you are forced to think in new and different ways.

5. *Improve your sense of humor.* This includes your ability to laugh at your own mistakes. Insightful and creative thinking is required to see the incongruities in a situation that makes something funny. Humor also helps reduce tensions, and you will be more creative when you are relaxed. (Humor is so important for magnetism that it receives separate attention in Chapter 8.)

6. *Adopt a risk-taking attitude when you try to find creative solutions.* You will inevitably fail a few times. One or two innovative ideas a year is sufficient to develop a reputation as a creative problem solver.

7. *Develop a creative mental set.* Allow the foolish side of you to emerge. Creativity requires a degree of intellectual playfulness and immaturity. Many creative people are accomplished practical jokers.

8. *Continually hunt for new ideas.* A creativity expert says, "I've worked with creative people in many industries, disciplines, and professions, and the really good ones are hunters. These people look outside their areas for ideas, and when they find an idea, they bring it back to their own area and apply it."[4]

9. *Identify the hours when you are at your creative best and attempt to accomplish most of your creative work during that period.* Most people are at their peak of creative productivity after ample rest, so try to work on your most vexing problem at the start of the workday. Schedule routine decision making and paperwork, and reviewing e-mail, when your energy level is lower than average.

10. *Be curious about your environment.* The person who routinely questions how things work (or why they do not work) is most likely to have an idea for improvement.[5]

You may have noticed that several of these ten suggestions support and reinforce the importance of overcoming traditional thinking. Repetition is important here because you need to approach from many directions the central task of becoming more innovative—increasing your mental flexibility.

Tell Anecdotes and Stories

Another potent way of projecting magnetism through language and thinking patterns is to make ample use of anecdotes and stories. Even when stories are not fascinating, they have a high human-interest value. Anecdotes and stories are a powerful technique for influencing others for several reasons. First, people like to hear anecdotes both from speakers and in face-to-face communications. Second, anecdotes help build the corporate culture, thus strengthening the organization. Third, workers can remember a principle or policy better if it is accompanied by an anecdote.

Most charismatic leaders make extensive use of anecdotes. Message-sending anecdotes relate to such subjects as a company president going out of his way to help an individual customer, or a lower-ranking employee who defied higher authority in order to meet her job responsibilities. In the latter instance, a receptionist at IBM denied admission to the company chairman, Tom Watson, because he was not wearing a security badge. Instead of firing the young woman, Watson praised her devotion to duty.

Several years ago, the Ford Motor Company announced far-reaching changes that would affect how cars were manufactured and how employees would work together. A senior Ford executive was chosen to deliver the closing remarks to a group of 300 Ford managers gathered to learn about the changes.

Toward the close of the speech, the executive told a story about Willie B., a formidable gorilla who lived for twenty-seven years in isolation in a dreary Atlanta zoo. He said that he had raised money for a state-of-the-art gorilla habitat. Willie B., for the first time in his life, would now live in a gorilla-friendly, close-to-natural environment. Yet somehow, Willie B. was slow to adapt to his new environment.

It took the gorilla several days to fully explore his new habitat. A photographer caught the moment when Willie B. tested the grass with a toe. The Ford executive hangs a framed photograph of this incident in his office. "It's there," he said, "to remind me that no matter how attractive the new surroundings might appear, it takes time and courage to leave the comfortable security of a place—even an ugly cramped space—that you know well."

At the moment the meeting ended, meeting participants came over to the speaker to express how much the speech had touched them. The story about the gorilla brought tears to the eyes of many. Of significance to the organization, many probably left the conference with an understanding of how difficult the coming changes were going to be for employees.[6]

Becoming an effective storyteller requires practice. However, the skill is well worth developing because of its contribution to a person's personal magnetism and leadership ability. Create a useful anecdote file of your own. Collect anecdotes about things you observe personally, those you hear from others, and those you read in books, magazines, and newsletters. Anecdotes can also be found in books and newsletters about speech making. Attempt to screen out those anecdotes that are widely used because stale anecdotes detract from magnetism. The accompanying insert contains a fresh anecdote about human disabilities and abilities.

What's a Disability?

A business professor had recently hired a new lawn service to cut the grass on his one-half acre property. After the first several cutting sessions, the professor met with the supervisor of the five-person crew to offer positive feedback on the crew's performance. The professor also made note of a remote corner on the lot that was being neglected. "No problem, we'll get that spot from here on out," said the supervisor.

The supervisor then casually mentioned, "Oh, by the way, two of my crew members are deaf kids from your college. They're real nice guys." The professor then asked how well the deaf workers were performing as lawn-care specialists.

The supervisor responded, "The two deaf guys are my best workers. They can follow instructions much better than the workers who can hear. With all the machinery going full blast, it's almost impossible to hear instructions. But the deaf guys can read my lips very well. Another advantage is that they don't have to lose work time by shutting off the machinery just to receive instructions. Since time is money in our business, every minute of productivity is important."

How might someone use the story about the deaf lawn-care specialists to enhance his or her magnetism and leadership effectiveness? The anecdote could be used to show the importance of valuing differences between workers. A manager might tell the story to illustrate the importance of appreciating the unique capabilities of people. Or the anecdote could be told to illustrate the point that under the right circumstances a weakness can be a strength, or a disability an ability.

Emphasize Positive Thoughts

A winning thought pattern of magnetic people is their propensity to express positive thoughts when it is appropriate to do so. Being grumpy limits a person's inspirational appeal. Changing a tendency toward being negative requires considerable discipline. This is true because people appear to have a biologically based predisposition to seeing either the positive or negative content in their lives. People are therefore apt to look at situations positively or negatively.

Nevertheless, even if you are a natural pessimist, you can learn to express optimism in the presence of others whom you want to influence positively. A few suggestions for the aspiring positive thinker are as follows:

1. *Frame negative messages in positive terms.* Suppose you are a retail store executive and you discover that your turnover rate is 40 percent per year. Your analysis is that such high turnover is too costly and creates customer service problems. You tell your store managers, "If we can reduce our turnover rate by just 10 percent we will beat the industry average, reduce costs, and improve customer satisfaction."

2. *Phrase scenarios in terms of what can be done or what will be done.* Similar to the suggestion just made, tell people how conditions can or will be improved. An inspiring leader would make a pronouncement such as, "If we can develop one new successful product this year, we can avoid a downsizing."

3. *Provide a clear-cut course of action.* In the example just mentioned, explain the action plan for developing a successful new product.

4. *Substitute positive terms for negative ones when feasible.* Examples include using the word *challenge* for *problem, major investment* instead of *major cost, developmental opportunity* for *personal weakness,* and the phrase *best suited for yesterday's challenges* when you want to avoid *obsolete.*

The most dynamic person must at times point out the true negatives in a situation. Yet even during the worst adversity, the magnetic individual will deliver a positive message about working out of this situation. A firm that counts coins for supermarkets and transit companies had filed for bankruptcy. Surrounding its bankruptcy was a question of approximately $1 million that appeared not to have been deposited in the customers' bank accounts.

The president told workers, "We have hit rock bottom, and I'm sure the newspaper accounts of what happened will not be rosy. Please do not despair. All the missing funds can be accounted for. We are going to stay in business, and we do not intend to lay off anyone. I'm as upset as anybody in this room. Let's stick together, and work our way back to health."

Use Positive Self-Talk

You no doubt have heard about the power of positive thinking. Closely related is the idea of making positive statements about yourself to enhance your magnetism. Positive self-talk basically involves saying positive things about oneself to oneself. Positive self-talk in front of others has the most immediate payoff in terms of being magnetic.

In the systematic method recommended here, the first step in using positive self-talk is to objectively state the incident that is causing you doubt about your self-worth.[7] The key word here is *objectively*. Melissa, who is fearful of poorly executing a customer-survey assignment, might say: "I've been asked to conduct a customer survey for the company, and I'm not good at conducting surveys."

The next step is to objectively interpret what the incident *does not* mean. Melissa might say, "Not being skilled at conducting a survey doesn't mean that I cannot figure out a way to do a useful survey, or that I'm an ineffective employee."

Next, you should objectively state what the incident *does* mean. In doing this, you should avoid put-down labels such as "incompetent," "stupid," "dumb," "jerk," or "airhead." All these terms are forms of negative self-talk. Melissa should state what the incident does mean: "I have a problem with one small aspect of this job, conducting a customer survey. This means I need to acquire skill in conducting a survey."

The fourth step is to objectively account for the cause of the incident. Melissa could say, "I'm really worried about conducting an accurate survey because I have very little experience of this nature."

The fifth step is to identify some positive ways to prevent the incident from happening again. Melissa might say, "I'll buy a basic book on conducting surveys and follow it carefully," or "I'll enroll in a seminar on conducting consumer surveys."

The final step is to use positive self-talk. Melissa imagines her boss saying, "This survey is really good. I'm proud of my decision to select you to conduct this important survey." When the opportunity arises, Melissa will say to her boss something to this effect: "I'm glad you asked me to conduct the survey. I'm eager to take on new challenges, and I've done well with them in the past." Or she might say to her boss, "Thanks for the opportunity for professional growth." This last statement is excellent for generating personal magnetism.

Making frequent positive statements about, or affirmations of, the self creates a more confident person and projects a positive image. When your ratio of positive self-statements to negative ones is very high, say, twenty-five to one, others will perceive you as a stronger, more confident person. However, if you never make negative self-statements (for example, "Sorry, I goofed on this one"), you will appear pompous and self-centered.

Display Bilingualism

A success factor in today's workplace is to have a good working knowledge of a second language and culture. An increasing number of managers who make it to the top of organizations speak, read, and write a second language well. Furthermore, many European managers speak three languages. In addition to bilingualism enhancing your chances for success, displaying your second-language skills adds to your magnetism. People are very impressed by an American who knows another language. In most other countries, knowing a second language is expected of most workers who have contact with customers or clients.

Considerable self-discipline and practice is required to become conversant in another language. Traditional thinking suggests that a second language can only be learned through several time-consuming routes. The standard ones are taking a course, studying it in books, and listening to video- and audiocassettes, buttressed by lengthy stays in the target country. You can also learn a second language by incorporating it into your daily life, using snippets of time as follows:

- *While driving, comment to yourself in your target language about what is happening around you.* For example, "It's warm," "The traffic is heavy," "I see a big truck," or "A police car is chasing after me."
- *While removing items from your shopping cart, refer to each by its name in your target language.*
- *Carefully study the instructions for film and videocassettes, and for household appliances that are written in several languages.* Here is a

natural opportunity to practice your second language because the translation has been done for you.

• *Team up with a family member or friend and have one or two meals a week in which you speak only your second language.* Your mother tongue is absolutely not allowed. How do you think your great-grandparents learned to speak English?

• *Devote 20 percent of your reading time to reading material in your second language.* Scientific, medical, and business data have many similarities regardless of the language in which they appear.

• *Write two postcards per week in your second language.* Your friends will laugh, and appreciate it even if they do not know your second language.

• *Purchase a cable TV or satellite hookup so that you can view people speaking your second language.* Thousands of foreigners learn their second language in this way.

• *Pay somebody who speaks the target language fluently to have a ten-minute telephone conversation with you each week.* No mother tongue allowed—just like the foreign dinner.

• *Patronize a restaurant that features food from your target culture.* Read the menu carefully and greet the proprietor, who probably speaks the foreign language of interest to you.

• *Speak to your pet, or your neighbor's pet, in your second language only.* Animals are nonjudgmental and will never laugh or criticize when you make a mistake. You will therefore be able to speak in your second language without feeling self-conscious.

In this chapter we have run through various strategies for displaying personal magnetism through language and thinking patterns. As a quick review, keep these strategies in mind:

1. Use colorful expressions and slogans.
2. Offer penetrating insights.
3. Express imaginative thoughts.
4. Tell anecdotes and stories.
5. Emphasize positive thoughts (including positive self-talk).
6. Display bilingualism.

You are now prepared to develop another major strategy for enhancing your personal magnetism—making effective use of emotional expressiveness.

3

Achieving Magnetism Through Emotional Expressiveness

Magnetic and charismatic individuals are more emotionally expressive than their less-inspiring counterparts. Furthermore, emotional expressiveness contributes to a person's ability to effectively use other magnetic behaviors such as flattering people or injecting humor into situations. People who tightly control their emotions rarely attract the attention of others. Note that I use the word *rarely*, not *never*. In rare instances an emotionally flat individual can be magnetic by effective use of other characteristics and behaviors, such as devotion to work or being highly considerate.

Given that emotional expressiveness makes such an important contribution to personal magnetism, I am going to describe several different approaches to enhancing your emotional effectiveness. Although a person's ability to effectively display emotion is an ingrained pattern of behavior, constructive changes are possible. An emotionally flat person can learn to be more expressive. And people whose unbridled emotional displays lead them to tune out others can learn to exercise more control.

Analyze Your Emotional Behavior and Handwriting

A starting point in effectively managing your emotional expressiveness is to take stock of your present level of emotionality. Two convenient methods of doing so are (1) to examine your past behavior and (2) to examine your handwriting. Both can be tip-offs to your basic level of emotionality.

Analyzing Your Emotional Behavior

A starting point in understanding your present level of emotional expressiveness is to think through the experiences you have had in expressing your feelings to others. Your behavior with respect to specific incidents can be more revealing than simply making a self-judgment such as "I am a highly emotional person" or "I am not an emotional person." To gain some insight into your present level of emotional expressiveness, take the accompanying self-quiz.

The Emotional Expressiveness Scale

Indicate how well each of the following statements describes you by circling the number under the best answer: very inaccurately (**VI**); inaccurately (**I**); neutral (**N**); accurately (**A**); very accurately (**VA**).

	VI	I	N	A	VA
1. While watching a movie, I sometimes shout out in laughter or approval.	1	2	3	4	5
2. During a group meeting, I occasionally show my approval by shouting "Yes" or "Fantastic."	1	2	3	4	5
3. During a group meeting, I have occasionally expressed disapproval by shouting out "Absolutely not" or "Horrible."	1	2	3	4	5
4. Several times while attending a meeting, someone has said to me, "You look bored."	5	4	3	2	1
5. Several times while attending a social gathering, someone has said to me, "You look bored."	5	4	3	2	1
6. Many times while at social gatherings or business meetings, people have asked me, "Are you falling asleep?"	5	4	3	2	1

	VI	I	N	A	VA
7. I thank people profusely when they do me a favor.	1	2	3	4	5
8. It's not unusual for me to cry at such events as weddings, graduation ceremonies, or engagement parties.	1	2	3	4	5
9. Reading about or watching on TV sad news events, such as an airplane crash, brings tears to my eyes.	1	2	3	4	5
10. When I was younger I got into more than my share of physical fights or shouting matches.	1	2	3	4	5
11. I dread having to express anger toward a co-worker.	5	4	3	2	1
12. I have cried among friends more than once.	1	2	3	4	5
13. Other people have told me that I am affectionate.	1	2	3	4	5
14. Other people have told me that I am cold and distant.	5	4	3	2	1
15. I can get so excited watching a sports event that my voice is hoarse the next day.	1	2	3	4	5
16. It is difficult for me to express love toward another person.	5	4	3	2	1
17. Even when alone, I will sometimes shout in joy or anguish.	1	2	3	4	5
18. Many people have complimented me on my smile.	1	2	3	4	5
19. People who know me well can easily tell what I am feeling by the expression on my face.	1	2	3	4	5
20. More than once, people have said to me, "I don't know how to read you."	5	4	3	2	1

Score _______

Scoring and Interpretation: Add the numbers you have circled, and use the following as a guide to your level of emotionality with respect to personal magnetism:

90–100 Your high level of emotionality could be interfering with your personal magnetism. Many others may interpret your behavior as being out of control emotionally.

70–89 Your level of emotionality is about right for a personally magnetic individual. Your are emotionally expressive, yet your level of emotional expression is not so intense as to be bothersome to others.

20–69 Your level of emotionality is probably too low to enhance your magnetism. To become more personally magnetic you will have to work hard at expressing your feelings to others.

Analyzing Your Handwriting

Here's a chance to be your own graphologist. A person's handwriting is one of the best clues to his or her level of emotionality. Since you know you will be analyzing your handwriting, it could influence the sample you produce. It would therefore be more objective to locate an already-existing sample of your handwriting. You will need more than your signature. A handwritten note would be best. If you do not have such a note available, substitute a To Do list or a shopping list. If you have neither available, handwrite a paragraph about anything, using words of different lengths.

Now carefully observe your handwriting, attempting to be objective, detached, and clinical. Here is your interpretive guide:

• *Emotional constriction*. People who are low in emotional expressiveness tend to have handwriting that is quite small, with tiny, precisely inscribed lettering. People with this style of handwriting typically squeeze in an average of twelve words to a line. Such writing is often—but not invariably—neat and easy to decipher. A sample of handwriting that reflects emotional constriction is presented next. How does your handwriting compare?

I want to be wealthy and happy.

• *Emotional expressiveness*. The handwriting of emotionally expressive individuals is large, expansive, and flowery. The letters are tall and wide, and the person typically writes about seven words per line. Emotionally expressive people make frequent use of exclamation points. Handwriting that is highly legible despite its expansiveness suggests good organization and work habits combined with high emotionality. A sample of emotionally expressive handwriting follows:

I want to be wealthy and happy.

• *Moderate emotional expressiveness.* Moderate emotionality is more difficult to diagnose through handwriting than are low or high emotionality. People with high, average, or low emotionality might have handwriting of an intermediate size. Small and large handwriting, as described above, tell more about a person's emotionality than does intermediate-size handwriting.

A logical question is: Will changing my handwriting change my emotional expressiveness? The answer is a resounding no. Changing your handwriting will not change your level of emotionality. The reverse is truer: As a person becomes more emotionally expressive, some of this increased expressiveness may lead to more open, less constricted handwriting.

Articulate Your Feelings

Now that you have given careful thought to your level of emotionality, you are in a position to judge how much development you need to become more emotionally expressive. There are far more people in business who need to enhance their emotional expressiveness level than there are people who need to tame it. Yet people who give free rein to their emotions may need to learn to express them in a constructive way that attracts people.

You must first become aware of your feelings in order to develop the ability to express them in a beneficial way. In general, people do not have much trouble making facts known to other people. It is your interpretation of those facts (your feelings and attitudes) that may create the problem. It is easier to say to a work associate, "You promised me your input by today," than to say, "I'm disappointed that you did not follow through on your commitment to give me your input by today." Maybe you shouldn't be disappointed but these are your feelings. (Personally magnetic people are able to candidly express both positive and negative feelings.)

To supplement your statements of fact, you must identify the feelings associated with the fact. The feeling points to an internal reaction you have to a person, event, or thing. Suppose you are trying to apply new software to a work problem. After one hour of trying, the software does the job you want it to do. The facts surrounding the event might include such ideas as the following:

> "It took one hour for me to get the software to run right."
>
> "I stuck with the job, and I was finally successful."
>
> "I worked my way through the task without asking a computer expert to help me."
>
> "I fell behind in my work because I spent so much time playing with the software."
>
> "I learned a new skill that will help me when I face a similar problem in the future."

All of the above are accurate factual statements that may reflect intelligence and good problem-solving ability. Yet they do not express the *feelings* surrounding the event. If you can identify your feelings in everyday events such as these, you have taken a giant first step toward becoming more emotionally expressive. Here are some of the feelings, along with the facts, that are most likely to be associated with the above events:

> "I'm so frustrated that it took me an hour to get the software to run right."
>
> "I'm elated. My persistence paid off. After sticking with the job, I was finally successful."
>
> "I'm so proud. I worked my way through the task without asking a computer expert to help me."
>
> "I'm so upset. I fell behind in my work because I spent so much time playing with the new software."

"I'm excited. I learned a new skill that will help me when I face a similar problem in the future."

To develop skill in recognizing your feelings, reflect on daily events and concentrate on your internal sensations. You will know you have identified a valid feeling if an internal sensation does arise after identifying the feeling. Here are two examples:

1. You have completed a ten-page report for your boss, replete with graphics and covered in a slick binder. If you say to yourself, "I love the looks of my report," you know you have identified a valid feeling if your body feels as if it is in a state of arousal. If you don't really feel anything approaching intense delight, the state of arousal will be lacking.

2. You are sitting in a meeting and the person next to you cracks his knuckles repeatedly. You say to yourself, "I wish he would stop. Knuckle cracking *distracts* me." You experience almost no internal reaction. You try again and say, "I wish he would stop. Knuckle cracking *nauseates* me." You experience nausea. Good job. You have correctly identified your feelings.

After developing skill in identifying your feelings to yourself, the next step is to practice expressing them to others. A general strategy is to reinforce many of the factual statements you make with the feelings behind them. Feelings such as those expressed in the examples given would have to be expressed to others as well as to yourself. Here are a few examples of the ways in which personally magnetic people might reinforce facts with feelings in speaking to others:

"You put in ten hours of your personal time to complete the project. It *excites* me that you care so much about the company."

"You shipped us a low-quality component, and it really *upsets* me. You have jeopardized the trust I had in you as a supplier."

"We cut our expenses without laying off people or sacrificing quality. I want to share my *delight* with you."

Another aspect of articulating your feelings is to express them directly rather than indirectly. Many people express their feelings in an indirect manner instead of explaining how they really feel about an event, person, or thing. Others attack something that is not the real issue. One example is a husband who berates his wife for being late in getting ready for an office party when what he is really upset about is that he dislikes the way his wife looks that evening.

A more direct and mutually beneficial approach might have been for him to say to his wife, "I must tell you that I do not care for the dress you have chosen for tonight. My feelings are that this dress does not do justice to your appearance. It upsets me that the dress makes you look matronly."

Another human tendency is to attack a general situation instead of being honest with ourselves about our feelings. A professional worker might say, "I hate this company. It's so dull. Nothing exciting is happening." If she expressed her true feelings, she would say, "I'm feeling discouraged and depressed. I've worked here for three years, and nobody has singled me out as a fast tracker. I'm not getting the recognition I think I deserve."

There are several rewards that come from expressing your true feelings directly. Your mental outlook improves, you appear more magnetic, and you are better able to deal with the problem. In the example just given, if the woman admitted to herself that her negative feelings stemmed from going unrecognized—not the dullness of the company—she could take remedial action. She might develop a plan for getting noticed.

Here are three more examples of the difference between direct and indirect expression of feelings. In the third example, you decide which are the direct and indirect alternatives.

1. *Indirect:* "Economic forecasts are a waste of time. They never really help us in our business."

   Direct: "I feel frustrated because I'm not confident of my abilities to apply economic forecasts to our business."
2. *Direct:* "I'm worried about not making my quota."

   Indirect: "The quotas imposed on us this month are unreal."
3. __________*:* "I thought learning to develop personal magnetism was something a person could do in a weekend."

   __________*:* "It's overwhelming to know that I would have to change a whole bunch of habits to become personally magnetic."

Exhibit Passion

A defining characteristic of personally magnetic people is the passion they have for other people and their work. Personally magnetic business owners love their customers and their employees. Personally magnetic performers love their art or sport. And personally magnetic team leaders are passionate about their teams and the work their teams are producing.

The passion we refer to contributes directly to a feeling of love. U.S. Army Major General John H. Stanford once told a team of leadership researchers:

> The secret to success is to stay in love. Staying in love gives you the fire to really ignite other people, to have a greater desire to get things done than other people. A person who is not in love doesn't really feel the kind of excitement that helps him or her to get ahead and lead others and to achieve. I don't know any other fire, any other thing in life that is more exhilarating and is more positive a feeling than love.[1]

To add passion as another contributor to personal magnetism, you need to find something to be passionate about, and then let others know of your passion.

Identify an Object of Your Passion

Perhaps you are fortunate enough to be passionate about another individual in your family or personal life. If not, think back to a time when you did experience passion for another person. You might be passionate by nature, but your passion was not released until it was ignited by another person. The same principle holds for the workplace and for pastimes. You need to find a passion-object to ignite whatever passion lies inside you.

Suppose you are not a highly passionate person by nature. It then becomes even more important for you to search for potential passion-objects in your work. With some digging and careful reflection, most people can find something to arouse their passion. The process involves a question of taking a careful inventory of the various components of your work, then identifying the elements that create the most excitement for you. Search for answers to the following questions:

- What part of my work would I be most willing to do while on vacation?
- As I begin to go to sleep or take a nap, what part of my work can I visualize that will put me in a tranquil frame of mind?
- What part of my work am I proud to talk about with friends and neighbors?
- What part of my work would I like to continue after retirement?
- What part of my work do I have the least difficulty concentrating on?
- Aside from the income, what part of my work would I miss the most if I were laid off or placed on disability?

You may not be able to find an answer to all these questions. An accurate response to even one of these questions, however, could place you on the road to passion and commitment. When performing chores other than your passion-object, you can think to yourself, "Soon I will be doing what I really love about this job."

Robyn Holden, the founder of Emergency 911 Security in Washington, D.C., is a germane example of identifying a passion-object. Holden maintains that she is earning a good living from her work, but her love for what she does is more important than the money. The company designs and installs security systems for commercial, federal, and residential clients.

Holden has found a sustaining source of passion in her work. She loves the gratification she receives from ensuring customer safety. "I know I'm protecting people," she says. "I'm saving people's lives. I'm giving them the opportunity to develop a comfort level within their businesses or within their homes."[2] Even if Holden is less excited about such business details such as ensuring that invoices are collected and bills are paid, she always has the passion of providing security clearly in mind.

Let Others Know of Your Passion

To be silently passionate about certain aspects of your work contributes to personal magnetism because others are attracted to dedicated people. You gain much more magnetism mileage, however, if you let others know of your passion. Your magnetism will shine through if you take the opportunity to let work associates and people outside the company know of your passion for your work.

A dentist I know attracts a steady stream of new patients in large part because he is so passionate about doing restorations and crowns. As he inserts a crown, he will say, "A work of art," "I'm getting better with age," and "Isn't this a fabulous piece of work?"

The passion this dentist displays for his work helps him in several ways. First, his passion enables him to perform work of the highest quality, thus leading to more crowns for his current patients. Second, he gets a large number of referrals from the same patients. Word of mouth works especially well in dentistry.

To get you in the right frame of mind for expressing work passion publicly, think about these examples:

- Steve Jobs, co-founder of Apple Computer Corporation and of two other high-tech companies since then (and now reaffiliated with Apple), would excite others with statements such as, "We are making outrageously good computers that will change the entire world."
- Tom Williams, a professor of statistics, tells his students on the first day of class, "You are about to take the most important course in your life. Here you will learn how to think and make decisions."
- Tammy Martino, the proprietor of a bakery that can barely keep up with demand for its baked goods, makes such statements to customers as, "I'm as happy baking a cake for your wedding as I would be in baking a cake for my own daughter's wedding," and "If I knew I were eating my last meal on earth, I would choose bread and dessert from my own bakery."
- A sales representative tells a customer, "I have had so much fun putting together this proposal for you because I know it will help your business enormously."
- You are attending a meeting in which you will be presenting. You tell the other participants, "It's hard to describe how enjoyable it was putting this plan together. I know it will work for us."
- You happen upon a creative idea, and then tell your team members, "I've discovered something that I am confident will take us to new heights. Let me share my excitement with you."

• You say to others from time to time, "I think I have one of the best jobs in the world. I'm helping people, and I love my work."

In each of these examples, the key person makes a statement that refers directly to an exuberant love of the task. Such statements have a big payoff in terms of projecting magnetism.

Make Tactical Use of Emotional Displays

Another mechanism for achieving personal magnetism through emotional expressiveness is to make tactical use of your emotional displays. By showing your feelings for effect (or using affect for effect), you are using them in a tactical, planned manner. However, if you simply throw tantrums that are beyond your control, you are not making tactical use of emotional displays. Larry Bossidy, the magnetic CEO of AlliedSignal referred to earlier, has mastered the art of using emotional display to advantage.

Although Bossidy is not overpaid in comparison to other executives holding similar responsibility, the issue of his pay surfaces at many meetings with workers. Bossidy tackles the issue head-on, with a hard-hitting emotional display. He says to the assembly of employees, "I never dreamed I'd make this much, but the market for CEOs got hot. Some of you will find that satisfactory, some won't."

At one time he stood in his shirtsleeves on a truck loading dock above a feisty group of workers, reacting to their gripes. "Do you deserve your pay?" yelled one supervisor. "Yes!" bellowed Bossidy, "Do you deserve yours?"[3]

By his display of emotion without losing control of the situation, Bossidy reinforced his stature as an imposing leader. The question "Do you deserve yours?" put the supervisor in his place without insulting him, yet it helped to get others to think through the issue of who deserves how much pay.

The emotions displayed for effect can be negative or positive. Table thumping works because it shows people you are serious, and triggers an emotional response in them. For example, table thumping may trigger memories in some of times when they upset their parents or other authority figures. Others observing the table thumping may experience a positive feeling of being controlled because they have stepped out of line. As primitive as table thumping might appear, it conveys the message that the thumper is formidable.

Cheering wildly, bursting into laughter, or crying with joy can all boost your magnetism and leadership effectiveness. People react to your emotion with an emotional reaction of their own. The significant point is that unless you elicit an emotional response from others, they will not be drawn to you.

Although the tactical use of emotional display is an effective technique of interpersonal influence, not everyone is equipped to use this technique. Some skill is involved in the tactical display of emotions. It requires substantial self-control and restraint. You also have to be aware of the effect you want to have on others, such as provoking sympathy for your cause.[4] The following suggestions will help you make effective use of emotional display:

- *Save emotional displays for rare occasions.* Otherwise you will appear to be emotionally immature and thus a poor model for others. Emotional displays are particularly effective when they stand in sharp contrast to a person's usual demeanor. Remember that you can still be emotionally expressive without having peaks of emotional displays. The combination of being generally emotionally expressive and displaying emotional peaks contributes heavily to magnetism.

- *Be explicit about your feelings.* Make statements such as "I'm so disappointed that we missed our target again" or "I feel incredibly good that we produced 40 percent beyond what anybody imagined we would."

- *Concentrate intently to get your nervous system aroused to a pitch that matches your emotion.* For example, if your eyes widen and blood rushes to your skin when you are screaming you will be more effective than if you don't feel angry inside.

- *Practice showing positive and negative emotion even when you don't feel that way inside.* A magnetic individual can press the toggle switch for emotional displays as needed.

- *Rehearse your emotional displays.* Take videos of yourself engaging in both positive and negative emotional displays. Before filming, have one or two workplace scenarios in mind in which an emotional display would be plausible. Even if you are not skilled at acting, you will benefit from the opportunity to manage your emotions.

I have been referring primarily to sudden displays of emotion to produce a dramatic effect. Another tactical use of emotional display can also enhance personal magnetism. Frequent smiling, even when your inner mood does not warrant a smile, is the most basic tactical use of emotional display. Smiling in the workplace has many known advantages. People who smile frequently are:

- More likely to be hired
- Less likely to be fired
- More likely to receive good performance reviews
- More likely to be perceived positively by customers
- More likely to receive higher tips than servers who smile less often
- More likely to be nominated for supervisory positions

Too much false smiling, however, has the striking disadvantage of being bad for your mental and physical health. People who are forced to smile for prolonged periods of time are more likely to engage in maladaptive behavior such as drug and alcohol abuse. In one study it was shown that service personnel who felt forced to engage in phony smiling even suffered from sexual dysfunction.[5]

To minimize the problems associated with false smiling, focus on some factor in a situation that warrants a smile, then respond to that situation with a smile. As a leader, for example, you might be discouraged by the negative attitudes some employees displayed during a crisis. You might be amused, however, by how childlike and self-defeating their behaviors were.

Make Inspirational Appeals

To be a leader, whether via one's formal position or by means of personal appeal, one has to inspire others to accomplish worthwhile goals. A natural method of inspiring others is to appeal to their emotions. A manager might say, for example, "If you are at all patriotic, you will want to make our product successful in the international marketplace." Emotions and feelings must be aroused before people take significant action. A technician might strive to do excellent work, but only after his or her need for pride or recognition has been stirred.

Successful executives make frequent use of inspirational appeals, as exemplified by David W. Johnson, the CEO of Campbell Soup Company. Several years ago during a company meeting held in a cafeteria, Johnson was exhorting employees to outdistance the competition. He strode across the stage, jabbing his fist into the air and sporting his Cheshire cat grin. In a loud voice he told employees, "Poor old Borden was bought by KKR and cut up like firewood. Anheuser-Busch couldn't even sell Eagle Snacks. Earnings decimated! Disaster! Death!"

Johnson's performance that day was typical for him. He has been described as having both the flair of an actor and the fervor of an evangelist. His showmanship was considered a major contributor to the renewed vigor of Campbell Soup after he arrived on board.[6]

Let's look at a variety of the techniques you can use to inspire others in the workplace. The same techniques, however, might also be used in community settings and to some extent within the family circle. To inspire others you will have to rely heavily on your own emotional expresssiveness.

Identify What You Want People to Do or Feel

A starting point in making an inspirational appeal is to identify what you want people to do or feel. You would then choose words, phrases, and ideas that fit your goal. As a manager you might be discouraged by the lax attitude employees have toward workplace cleanliness and housekeeping. Your goal is for the workers to maintain a near-spotless work area. Your inspirational appeal to fit the situation might then include such comments as:

> "How would you people like to start looking like winners?"
>
> "A neighbor of mine visited our Japanese competitor last week.

> He couldn't help noticing that the factory looked as clean as a dealer showroom."
>
> "If we want others to think we are professionals, we have to start looking like professionals."

Notice that when Johnson of Campbell Soup was attempting to inspire people to overwhelm the competition, he zeroed in on the problems the competition was experiencing. In this way his employees might feel that the goal of outdistancing the competition was attainable.

Make an Appeal to Strong Values

A basic tactic for inspiring others is to trigger thoughts related to strong values. Appealing to strong values is important because it leads to commitment to the tasks on the part of others. Among these strong values in the workplace are:

- Being the best
- Outperforming the competition
- Squeezing out high profits
- Providing opportunities for employees
- Company loyalty
- Enhancing one's status
- Being a good corporate citizen

To enhance your magnetic appeal in the situation, explicitly mention, or allude to, these values in your appeal. You might say to group members, for example, "I know you folks want to be the best," or "I have an idea that will lead to increased opportunities for all of us."

Ask the Right Questions

An effective inspirational technique is to ask people questions that result in emotion-provoking answers. Your questions prompt others to give answers that stir their emotions and lead them to action. The question asked earlier in this chapter, "How would you people like to start looking like winners?" is a good example.

Asking a question is often better than simply saying, "I would like you people to start acting like winners." The reason is that answering a question results in more mental activity and commitment than just listening to a message does.

The *right question* depends on the values, needs, aspirations, and dreams of the people being asked. Nevertheless, here are a few questions that stand a good chance of being right (stirring emotion and being inspirational) in workplace situations:

- "Do you want to earn enough money to be financially secure?"
- "How many more times do you want our group to be singled out for having the worst quality record in the company?"
- "How would you feel about being number one?"
- "When are we going to stop fixing blame and start fixing problems?"
- "What can you do today to make our company a better place to work in?"

Appeal to Multiple Senses

Another tactic for making an inspirational appeal is to appeal to more than one sense. You want people to hear your message, but you also want them to see it, feel it in their muscles, touch it, and taste it. Encourage people to imagine the total experience of achieving the goal you believe is important. The manager facing an extraordinarily difficult deadline might inspire the group to achieve this goal with such statements as:

> "Can you imagine what it will *look* like to see 150,000 of these units packaged and loaded into trucks?"
>
> "Just think of how your family members will *squeal* with delight when you tell them you have earned a bonus equal to 10 percent of your annual salary."
>
> "We are on the way to our most profitable year in a decade. Join me in *tasting* victory."

"Imagine how *relaxed* your body will feel after we have achieved this momentous accomplishment."

"Just think of the *aroma* of the sumptuous food that will be served at our victory banquet after we hit our deadline."

Inspire People With Success Stories

In Chapter 2 I explained how magnetic people make frequent use of anecdotes and stories. Similarly, success stories are a natural way of inspiring others to extend themselves. Browse through media sources and books for stories about ordinary people who rose to great heights of achievement. People are often inspired by stories of individuals who began a business in their garage or kitchen and built it into a national or world-class leader. Every city contains citizens who have accomplished the equivalent of developing a barbecue sauce in their kitchens then, step by step, growing it into a product with nationwide distribution.

Use success stories as needed but do not use them so often that work associates and friends groan, "Ugh. Not another corny rags-to-riches tale."

In this chapter we have considered various approaches to achieving personal magnetism through being emotionally expressive, and also by appealing to the emotions of others. Focusing on emotions is a major component of becoming more magnetic because the perception of magnetism is based on an emotional reaction to an individual. As a quick review, remember these strategies and tactics:

1. Analyze your emotional behavior and handwriting.
2. Articulate your feelings.
3. Exhibit passion.
4. Make tactical use of emotional displays.
5. Make inspirational appeals. (Such appeals are important because they require you to be emotionally expressive.)

4

Projecting Magnetism Through Extraverbal Techniques

Personal magnetism requires much more than the effective use of language. Magnetic individuals communicate with their entire body, thus making effective use of extraverbal (or nonverbal) communication. You are undoubtedly familiar with nonverbal communication, or silent messages. The purpose of this type of communication is to help convey the feeling associated with a message. The slant here on extraverbal communication is to present those extraverbal techniques that will most likely contribute to your personal magnetism.

Learning to manipulate extraverbal techniques to enhance magnetism is challenging for two major reasons. One challenge is that extraverbal communication is imprecise. Even more so than words, a given extraverbal signal will not be interpreted in the same way by all those receiving the signal. Suppose you forcefully move your hand with the thumb extended in front of you, and then make a quick jerking motion upward. Most people observing you will interpret your gesture as an indicator of optimism and triumph. Consciously or unconsciously, your gesture will contribute to your image as a magnetic person in the minds of *most* of the people receiving your message.

Several of the people receiving your message, however, will interpret it differently, even negatively. Someone might say to himself, "Write off this character, he (or she) is acting like a silly teenager." Another person might think to herself, "Ugh! I can't stand a cliché in the form of a hand gesture."

To respond to this challenge, recognize that using nonverbal techniques to enhance your magnetism will not work with all those people you are trying to influence. A realistic goal of using nonverbal techniques is to increase the *odds* that you will have a magnetic effect on others.

Another challenge in using nonverbal techniques to enhance your magnetism is that considerable practice is required before a given signal will appear spontaneous. An unspontaneous, or stiff, nonverbal signal usually has a negative effect. Have you ever watched a speaker use hand gestures in such a way that it looks as if he had been told to use those gestures? The gestures probably appeared disconnected from the words being delivered. As a result, the nonverbal signals detracted from rather than enhanced the delivery.

To capitalize on the potential contribution of nonverbal signals to enhance your magnetism, you will need to practice them frequently enough so that they become smoothly blended into your repertoire. The practice required to master a magnetic nonverbal communication is yet another reminder that developing or enhancing magnetism is a tough, time-consuming assignment.

Our program for using extraverbal techniques to enhance magnetism is divided into two parts. First, you must learn to achieve congruence between your verbal and extraverbal signals and among your various extraverbal signals. Second, you must practice specific extraverbal indicators of magnetism even if each one does not communicate magnetism to all those you are attempting to influence.

Achieving Congruence in Your Messages

Extraverbal messages contribute mightily to the emotional impact of a message, and thus are closely linked to magnetism. The most important general principle for enhancing extraverbal effectiveness is to achieve congruence, or consistency, between the verbal and nonverbal parts of your message. Suppose you say to somebody, "I'm so sorry to hear about your job loss; tell me about it." At the same time, you have a concerned, saddened look on your face, and you squint intently. You sit in your chair as if you want to be there until the person has finished his or her story. You have achieved congruence, and you will come across as sympathetic, and perhaps magnetic.

Replay the same scenario. You make the same statement: "I'm so sorry to hear about your job loss; tell me about it." At the same time, you have a bored, distracted look on your face. You direct your gaze in several directions. You fidget in your chair, and your posture appears aimed at leaving the scene quickly. You are displaying incongruence, and you will leave the other person feeling flat and disappointed. Furthermore, that person will not be drawn closer to you; you have in fact scored a zero for personal magnetism.

An important general principle here is that you can strengthen your verbal messages by ensuring that your words and extraverbal language are consistent. When your verbal and extraverbal messages match, you convey the impression that you are honest and can be trusted. The listener in this scenario, for example, will believe that you are interested in his or her plight if your extraverbal message reinforces your verbal statement of concern.

Consistency between verbal and extraverbal messages contributes to magnetism because the magnetic person is integrated and credible. To analyze the degree of your consistency between verbal and extraverbal messages, take the accompanying quiz.

The Consistency Quiz

The purpose of this quiz is to start you thinking about the consistency between your verbal and extraverbal messages, and also about the consistency among your various extraverbal messages. So that you can respond to the statements with a high degree of accuracy, you might want input from sources other than your own introspection. If feasible, videotape yourself in conversation with a friend, talking about an emotional topic such as your relationship with a significant other or your personal finances. Another key source of input would be to have a close friend or family member help you respond to the statements on the basis of his or her knowledge of you.

Respond to the following statements as being mostly true or

mostly false to the best of your knowledge. Do not be concerned that the most accurate answer to many of the statements maybe "It depends on the situation" or "It would be difficult for me to judge." Force yourself to choose between "mostly true" and "mostly false" so that any important trend in your behavior can be uncovered.

	Mostly True	**Mostly False**
1. When I discipline another person, I sometimes laugh.	______	______
2. While making love I tend to daydream about work, sports, or household chores.	______	______
3. I often say "Have a nice day" while I am preoccupied with another thought.	______	______
4. When I express anger, I can feel my entire body becoming tight.	______	______
5. When I smile at another person, my entire body feels relaxed.	______	______
6. At times I cheer at a public event even if I'm feeling depressed.	______	______
7. Sometimes I laugh so hard that I have the urge to urinate.	______	______
8. I sometimes smile and nod my head during a meeting even when I'm feeling tense about wasting time or boredom.	______	______
9. When I'm conversing with another person, I sometimes lose my train of thought because I'm thinking of something else.	______	______
10. I will sometimes cry at an emotional event such as a funeral or wedding even when I am not touched by what is happening.	______	______
11. Sometimes when I have an orgasm during sex with another person, I will shout in ecstasy in an exaggerated manner.	______	______
12. I often express my anger by speaking in a low voice and flat tone.	______	______
13. I have heard more than once that my eyes look happy when I laugh.	______	______

	Mostly True	Mostly False
14. When I pay people compliments, they often have a perplexed look on their face.	______	______
15. I often scratch my head or touch my chin when working on a difficult problem.	______	______
16. When I tell people that I'm upset or angry, they often don't take me seriously.	______	______
17. When I'm in an intense discussion with another person, I experience physiological symptoms like sweating under my arms or breathing faster.	______	______
18. More than once while I was smiling, someone said to me, "Are you sure you are having a good time?"	______	______
19. I often get headaches while others think I'm having a wonderful time.	______	______
20. When I'm listening to another person, I usually think of absolutely nothing else.	______	______

Score ____________

Scoring: Give yourself a plus one for each response that agrees with the suggested answer in the congruent direction. The answer key that follows also explains the justification for each answer in the congruent direction.

1. *Mostly false.* Laughing is generally not consistent with disciplining another person unless it is done to relieve tension.
2. *Mostly false.* A person with high congruency concentrates intensely on the task at hand.
3. *Mostly false.* The congruent person minimizes making automatic statements that do not reflect what he or she is really feeling.
4. *Mostly true.* To convey a strong emotion like anger, a congruent person would have many parts of the body in synch.
5. *Mostly true.* A smile is a relaxing experience that should be reflected through the entire body, indicating congruence between facial expression and other parts of the body.
6. *Mostly false.* Cheering while depressed is an example of incongruence that would detract from the authenticity of the act.

7. *Mostly true.* A highly authentic laugh would create physiological reveberations throughout the involuntary nervous system.
8. *Mostly false.* It may be admirable to smile and nod while tense from the boredom and apparent waste of time, yet the smiling and nodding would lack authenticity.
9. *Mostly false.* A highly congruent person concentrates intensely so as to become highly involved in the moment.
10. *Mostly false.* A highly congruent person will show a correspondence between feelings and overt actions such as crying.
11. *Mostly false.* Exaggerating the intensity of an orgasm by shouting loudly is an extreme act of incongruence. Furthermore, your faking may become transparent to your partner.
12. *Mostly false.* A few people can express anger by lowering their voice level and speaking in a monotone, but most congruent people will at least modify their tone.
13. *Mostly true.* Happy-looking eyes while laughing are an excellent example of congruency.
14. *Mostly false.* The perplexity people show probably reflects a lack of authenticity in the compliment, as indicated by a frown or other negative facial expression.
15. *Mostly true.* Scratching one's head or touching one's chin when problem solving are good examples of extraverbal behavior being in synch with another aspect of behavior (in this case, thinking).
16. *Mostly false.* People are often not taken seriously because there is a poor match between what they are saying and their extraverbal behavior.
17. *Mostly true.* Although such physiological symptoms can simply be stress indicators, they also show a congruence between thought and behavior.
18. *Mostly false.* People will question whether someone is having a good time even though smiling when other extraverbal signs (such as body tightness) do not match the smile.
19. *Mostly false.* If others think you are having a good time, and you get headaches, your extraverbal behavior is not in synch with your feelings.
20. *Mostly true.* A congruent person concentrates intently.

Interpretation:

17–20 You show an unusually high degree of congruence that will contribute substantially to your personal magnetism.

9–16 You show an average degree of congruence that will neither add to nor particularly detract from your personal magnetism.

0–8 You have a below-average degree of congruence that could detract from your personal magnetism. Strive to get your verbal and extraverbal communication in synch.

Recognizing the importance of congruence in communication is an important first step in becoming more congruent. Keep in the back of your mind the goal of achieving congruence between your verbal and extraverbal communication. Your aim to is integrate your various ways of sending messages in order to appear more credible and magnetic. To repeat, people are more drawn to people who deliver congruent messages. There are several actions you can take that support the goal of achieving congruence. Engaging in the following behaviors can multiply the effectiveness of your communication:

1. When you tell others you are feeling relaxed or happy, or mention some other positive state, consciously relax your muscles and facial expression.

2. When you are trying to convince someone that you are well motivated and energetic, speak at an above-average pace and make quick movements. Above all, avoid yawning or having a bored expression on your face.

3. When you ask another person to "tell me about your day (or vacation, new project, child, grandchild, hobby, spouse, boyfriend, girlfriend, or new computer)," gaze carefully at the person and widen your eyes. Leaning toward the person also supports your request, as does a quizzical, inquiring look. Minimize agitated behaviors such as scratching your face or tapping your feet. Also guard against the verbal behavior of quickly introducing another topic once the person begins talking.

4. When you say to another person, "I'm telling you the truth," or "I'm being absolutely candid with you," look at the person directly and do not lower your voice tone. It is also important to minimize inappropriate finger or foot tapping, shifting of the body, or putting your hand over your face.

5. If you tell someone "I understand very well what you are saying," avoid the following:
   a. Knitting your brow
   b. Having a deadpan expression on your face
   c. Slightly raising one eyebrow
   d. Saying "yes" or "I see" in a strained voice
   e. Murmuring "I understand" while looking away[1]

6. When you deliver an affirmation to another person, such as "We must have lunch" or "I'll call you," elevate or modulate the tone of your voice. Also, give at least a small smile and avoid a deadpan expression. If you have no intention of having lunch with the person or telephoning him or her, the flat tone and deadpan expression will communicate exactly what is on your mind.

Another strategy for achieving congruence is to concentrate carefully on your thoughts when communicating with others. Concentration is crucial for congruence because it allows you to align the rest of the nervous system with your brain. Let's begin with an extreme example: You are in the process of expressing enthusiasm for an idea developed by your teammates. As you begin to verbalize your enthusiasm, your attention is suddenly diverted to the electric range in your kitchen.

You think to yourself, "Good grief, I left the range on high when I left the house in a hurry. I also left a dish towel near the range. The heat could have set the towel on fire. The fire could have spread to the wall, and then to the rest of the house. Who can I call? What can I do? I'm stuck here in this meeting."

You can imagine the effect on your extraverbal language. It is difficult to convey enthusiasm with your facial expression and body language when you are worried about your house burning down. Magnetic people, as well as other high achievers, typically concentrate on the task or people at hand. In this way, the emotion being experienced is not diluted or diverted. If you want to communicate anger, do not get sidetracked by a pleasant sexual fantasy. If you want to express passion, do not get diverted by thinking of a recent event that angered you.

The dilution and diversion take place because when you have competing thoughts, your brain sends mixed messages to the rest of your nervous system. If you are attempting to express enthusiasm, your brain will be transmitting messages such as, "Loosen your muscles," "Smile," "Dilate your pupils," "Soften the expression in your eyes," and "Pump just a little extra blood to the surface blood vessels."

If your enthusiasm is diverted by negative thoughts (such as your house burning down or a recent automobile accident), your nervous system will also be sending out fright and panic messages to the rest of your body. Among them will be "Drain away blood from the face to use it for the internal organs," "Frown," "Bite your lips," "Grind your teeth," and "Stiffen your muscles."

Unless you are a remarkably good actor, it will be difficult to send congruent messages when you have incongruent thoughts. If you concentrate on one thought at a time, it will be easier to send congruent messages. Concentration is both a skill and a mental attitude. Unfortunately, concentration is required to improve your concentration! Nevertheless, here are several guidelines to help you improve your concentration:

- *Say to yourself silently, "I have to concentrate on one idea now. I will allow no interruptions."*
- *Imagine yourself wearing blinders.* Keep in mind that the purpose of the blinders is to block out extraneous thoughts. Blinders on horses, similarly, help them concentrate better on what is in front of them rather than being distracted by what they see with their peripheral vision.
- *If your concentration begins to wander, say to yourself, "Stop. Get back to what you were doing."*
- *Repeat to yourself periodically a phrase that highlights why you are interacting with people at the moment.* Examples include, "Get their approval," "Win their confidence," "Close the sale," "Get more budget," and "Get their commitment."
- *Before you get started interacting with people over a particular issue, say to yourself, "The only thing that matters right now is this meeting with these people."* If your attention begins to wane during the interaction, repeat the phrase.
- *Attempt to divide up (or compartmentalize) the various spheres of your life.* Make statements to yourself such as, "Right now I am in my work sphere," or "Right now I am in my parent sphere." These

statements will help you stay focused on the situation at hand. Without concentrating on one sphere of life at a time, the various roles you play will interfere with each other and make your communication incongruent. Interference is more pronounced when you have an unresolved problem in one sphere of your life. It is difficult to appear animated and congruent at the office when your creditors are sending you nasty messages on your e-mail.

The concentration we are talking about can also be framed as a strong internal focus. You know what you want to accomplish in your life, which leads to an understanding of what you want to accomplish each year, each month, each week, each day, each hour, and each minute. In this way, when you want to excite others with your passion for a new business plan, you are not diverted at this moment by your dissatisfaction with a smaller-than-expected bonus.

Achieving congruence is a major contributor to magnetism because incongruence consciously and unconsciously sends people away from rather than toward you. If we use the analogy to a physical magnet, incongruence literally *repels* rather than attracts people.

Specific Extraverbal Indicators of Magnetism

Achieving congruence between verbal and extraverbal behavior is a major contributor to personal magnetism. In addition, the various modes of nonverbal communication all contain opportunities for helping you to become a magnetic person. Each extraverbal indicator, even one as modest as making occasional chopping motions with your hand while speaking, is just one more small contributor to magnetism. Pick and choose among these extraverbal indicators of magnetism to add to your personal magnetism tool kit.

In selecting extraverbal indicators to enhance your personal magnetism, keep in mind that they will not all have a positive effect or even be noticed by everybody. Try a blend of these indicators, and hope that some will have their intended effect. A useful analogy is to imagine that you are an unattached person attempting to attract a partner. Every relationship begins with an opening line, if only the modest "Hello." If you want to increase your chances of making that once-in-a-lifetime contact, you will need to try dozens of opening lines, because no one line works for everybody you might want to attract. If you attempt enough plausibly effective opening lines, you increase your chances of getting to know someone.

Head, Face, and Eye Movements

When used in combination, the head, face, and eyes provide the clearest indication of attitudes toward other people. Because of this fact, the head, face, and eyes are important in expressing confidence and projecting magnetism. Moving your head, face, and eyes toward another person makes you appear more magnetic. As is well known, messages accompanied by eye contact are more favorably interpreted by receivers than are messages sent without eye contact.

Less well known is the fact that eye contact alone may improve the sending of messages but it is not necessarily a major contributor to magnetism. Warm, friendly eye contact is the best for magnetism. Creating warm eye contact is no easy task. To improve this subtle dimension of extraverbal behavior, make a videotape of somebody on television who maintains warm eye contact. Study the person's glance several times. To practice the person's warm eye contact, first visualize the expression in the person's eyes, then attempt to emulate it. The eye contact may appear warm in part because it is accompanied by a smile.

Some political analysts predict that New Jersey Governor Christie Whitman will run for the office of president in the year 2000 or 2004. Most people would perceive Whitman as polished, professional, and formidable. Yet her closest advisers agree that she would become even more magnetic if she projected more warmth via her head, face, and eye movements. Whitman sometimes appears too cool and controlled. She has been coached to smile more frequently during public appearances. After being coached on these aspects of extraverbal behavior in 1995, Whitman has made substantial progress. (To further enhance her magnetism, Whitman was also advised to add more anecdotes to her talks—as you were so advised earlier in this book.)

Posture

"Walk into your prospect's office straight and tall. Show that you represent the finest line of ball bearings in the world," shouted the sales manager of yesteryear. Observations made today by specialists in extraverbal communication support the sale manager's exhortation. Posture does communicate a message, and contributes to or detracts from magnetism. Leaning toward another individual suggests that you are favorably disposed toward the person and to what he or she has to say. Leaning backward indicates the opposite.

Openness of the arms or legs serves as an indicator of liking or caring, which in turn may contribute to magnetism. In general, people maintain closed postures (arms folded and legs crossed) when speaking to people they dislike. The magnetic individual severely restricts communicating dislike unless it is strategically advisable to do so, for instance, when intimidating an enemy.

Standing up straight (assuming a person is able-bodied) generally reflects high self-confidence and magnetism. Personally magnetic people rarely stoop or slouch when interacting with others.

Shrugging the shoulders is another aspect of posture that can contribute to magnetism. Accompanied by a warm facial expression, a shrug will often be interpreted as "I'm not entirely convinced, but why not give your idea a try?" The shrugger is therefore giving the other individual some encouragement.

A subtle indicator of the potential contribution of posture to magnetism is that people tend to overestimate the height of people they perceive to be magnetic. This positive distortion is usually of the magnitude of two inches. A physical factor contributing to this perception is that magnetic people typically stand up straight, thus appearing approximately two inches taller than their slouching counterparts.

Body Position and Interpersonal Distance

How far you stand from people you are attempting to influence or attract can shape their perceptions of your appeal. The *intimate distance zone* extends from actual physical contact to about eighteen inches. Standing in this zone could be interpreted as confidence or brashness, but you might also be perceived as too intimidating or harassing. Using the *personal distance zone* ranging from about one and one-half to four feet is generally best for projecting magnetism. I have noticed a tendency among magnetic individuals to get as physically close to others as possible without invading their personal space and creating discomfort.

Not moving closer than the personal distance zone helps prevent your being perceived as sexually harassing another individual—a perception the magnetic person would prefer to avoid. The risk of physical closeness being interpreted as harassment is less for women than it is for men. Several well-known women executives incorporate hugging and physical touching into their personal style. Anita Roddick, the widely mentioned founder of the Body Shop, is an active hugger in a business setting. She freely hugs and touches the natives she encounters in her worldwide forays to find product ideas.

Linda Marcelli, the director of the New York City district for Merrill Lynch, is another magnetic hugger. She greets colleagues and clients with hugs and sometimes kisses. Marcelli says, "If one of my financial consultants is having a problem, I'll put my arm around him."[2] Marcelli sees no problem in establishing physical contact with others in the workplace. It is one of her extraverbal methods of projecting warmth and caring.

Magnetic people who are huggers and touchers appear to have the sensitivity to hug and touch others in a way that is unlikely to be interpreted as sexual. For example, they tend to give sideways rather than direct, frontal hugs.

The *social-consultative distance zone* is about four feet to eight feet. Although some cool and reserved influential people stay in this zone, it could be interpreted as shying away from closeness with others, thus detracting from magnetism.

Hand Gestures

Gestures made with the hand provide a not-to-be-wasted opportunity for being perceived as magnetic and commanding. Consider these extraverbal possibilities for enhancing your magnetism:

- Punching a fist into the air to communicate the message "Let's do it!"
- Using a finger as a pointing rod to emphasize a point or to direct others.
- Open-palm slapping of another's hand to signify strong agreement or to offer congratulations.
- Extending the thumb upward to indicate strong approval.
- Extending the first two fingers after the thumb into a V, with the remaining two fingers folded, to symbolize victory.
- Extending both arms upward in a V-shape, with the first two fingers of each hand also in a V-shape, to indicate unity and victory.
- Frequent brief chops into the air with the hand about perpendicular to the floor to emphasize a point.
- Extending the palms toward the sky or ceiling while moving the four fingers on both hands toward you (like a parking attendant directing you to come closer) to indicate "Join me" or "Tell me more."
- Placing the upper arm close to the body and making small punches forward (like a prize fighter delivering a body punch during a clinch) to indicate strong agreement.
- Extending both palms forward (the same motion required for pushing a heavy object) to communicate forcefully the following message: "I don't want to hear any more of this."

A general purpose of hand gestures is as *illustrators* to add emphasis or to clarify a message. Examples of illustrators include pointing toward the floor while saying, "Our profits are nosediving," and punching your fist into an open palm while saying, "I know we can do better than this." Judicious use of illustrators contributes to the animation of personally magnetic individuals. The next time you observe an individual in person or on television whom you regard as magnetic or charismatic, carefully observe his or her use of illustrators.

Another way in which hand gestures can contribute to magnetism is when they are used as *affect displays* that communicate the emotion one is experiencing. Such displays are generally used in conjunction with other modes of extraverbal behavior, especially facial expressions. The recommendation is to use affect displays that enhance a perception of magnetism. One example is clenched fists to communicate tension. A product manager at Procter & Gamble says that she can always tell when her boss is disappointed with the quarterly results by the way he clenches his fists. "We get a chuckle because Sid's fists tighten long before he tells us he's not pleased."

Scratching the back of one's head usually suggests that a person is perplexed. This gesture may contribute to magnetism because it helps project an image of warmth and humility. A hand-over-mouth gesture usually indicates shock, surprise, or remorse, thus enhancing the human qualities of the person using the gesture.

Although the hand gestures just mentioned can contribute to magnetism, they must be combined with many of the other magnetic characteristics and behaviors described in this book. Many people whom almost nobody but immediate family members would consider magnetic use numerous hand gestures while talking. To reiterate my major theme, a host of small behaviors can contribute to magnetism, but no single behavior or characteristic in and of itself will make you personally magnetic.

Voice Quality and Tone

The manner in which a person speaks can contribute positively or negatively to a perception of magnetism. Often, more significance is attached to the *way* something is said than to *what* is said. A forceful voice, which includes a consistent tone without vocalized pauses, connotes power, control, and confidence, thus contributing to a perception of magnetism. A whispery, wimpy voice detracts from a person sounding confident and being able to take charge or to influence others.

Avoiding an annoying voice quality can have a positive impact on others. The research of voice coach Jeffrey Jacobi provides some useful suggestions. He surveyed a nationwide sample of 1,000 men and women, and asked, "Which irritating or unpleasant voice annoys you the most?" The answer was a whining, complaining, or nagging tone. Jacobi notes that we are judged by the way we sound. He also notes that careers can be damaged by an unpleasant voice. Jacobi continues: "We think about how we look and dress. And that gets most of the attention. But people judge our intelligence much more by how we sound than how we dress."[3]

The conclusion that voice quality contributes to or detracts from magnetism does not imply that there is no room for individuality in this dimension. A pleasant (magnetic) voice can encompass a wide range of regional accents. Many people would consider former business executive and Reform Party presidential candidate H. Ross Perot and financier Donald Trump as magnetic. Perot has a Texan good-old-boy quality to his voice, while Trump sports traces of the tough-talking New Yorker.

To improve your voice quality, try these do-it-yourself techniques:

- Listen to your voice on a tape cassette, videocassette, or voice-mail system. Keep repeating the same message until you are satisfied that you sound like a confident and magnetic person.
- While listening to your voice, search for common voice problems such as a monotonous tone, squeakiness, a too-thick accent, or tendencies to mumble or to talk too fast.
- Several times per week visualize yourself speaking to work associates and practice using the voice quality you think will convey the impression that you are personally magnetic.
- Consult a speech therapist or coach to help identify any facets of your voice that detract from your image.

Changing the quality of your voice dramatically would take years because one's voice is composed of so many ingrained, long-term habits. However, just by modifying a few of your worst habits you might be able to make noticeable improvements. For example, by learning to exaggerate your lip movements you could substantially reduce that mumbling quality that has been driving your friends crazy for years.

Personal Appearance

Everybody knows that one's external image communicates messages to others. People pay more respect and grant more privileges to those they perceive as being tastefully dressed and neatly groomed. The problem is that the nature of what constitutes an impressive appearance changes quickly. To use personal appearance to enhance magnetism, the general principle is to observe what trend is fashionable and then find a way to create flair for yourself within that trend.

If you are bold enough, you could try being a trendsetter. A stylish example is Anthea Disney, the editor-in-chief of News Corp./MCI Online Ventures. She has been known to wear a leather motorcycle-style jacket, along with a sweater dress, to the office. Disney claims that since people do not question her authority, she can come to work in such attire.[4] In the future, Disney will probably choose other styles that will support a casual, powerful look.

A danger in using clothing and appearance to enhance one's magnetism is that you might dress so elegantly that others will focus on your clothing rather than on you. For purposes of magnetism, it is better to draw attention to one's character, attitudes, and behavior than to one's appearance. At least in a work environment, wearing the most expensive clothing can detract from a person's more important qualities. However, a noteworthy appearance is a desirable goal. To add to your magnetic qualities, consider these desirable aspects of dress and appearance as worth having:

- Neatly pressed and sparkling-clean clothing
- Freshly polished shoes (an outstanding return on time and money in terms of making a favorable impression)
- Impeccable fingernails
- Appropriate jewelry in mint condition
- Well-maintained hair that nevertheless looks natural, not straight out of the beauty parlor or barbershop.
- Good-looking teeth of a white or antique white color
- A trace of cologne or perfume
- A modest amount of body piercing, but definitely not a pierced tongue, lip, or nose

Remember that clothing and appearance are important, but only as a supplement to more fundamental ways of being magnetic or charismatic. If magnetism were strictly related to clothing, thousands of retail store sales associates would be magnetic because a large percentage of these workers dress for success.

Use of Time

A subtle mode of extraverbal communication in the workplace is the use of time. Guarding time as a precious resource will help you project a powerful and magnetic image. A statement such as "I can devote twenty minutes to your problem this Thursday at 11:30" will make you appear confident and in control. Too many of these statements, however, might make you appear unapproachable and lacking in consideration. Instead of drawing people toward you because of your importance, you will create distance between yourself and others. Suggestions for projecting personal magnetism though the use of time include:

- Being prompt for meetings.
- Starting and ending meetings on time when you are the leader.
- Jotting down appointments in your day planner or electronic device in front of others.
- Making references to dates or years in the future, such as by reporting: "In 2002 the market value of our company stock should reach $1 billion."

Information technology has created new challenges in the use of time. If you are considerate enough to respond to all your e-mail messages, it will increase your attractiveness to many people. Yet if you have enough discretionary time to answer every e-mail message it could detract from your mystique. Similarly, you want to appear in touch with the modern world by talking about your forays into cyberspace. Yet if you have enough slack in your schedule to surf the Internet regularly, how valuable can your time be? Attempt to achieve a balance between being tuned into current information technology and not being so consumed that the importance of your time becomes suspect.

In summary, we have looked at two overall strategies for using extraverbal communication to enhance personal magnetism. The first strategy is to achieve congruence between your verbal and extraverbal messages. Your various extraverbal messages should also be congruent with each other. Concentration is a major contributor to consistency. In quick review, the categories of extraverbal communication that should be managed well to enhance personal magnetism are as follows:

1. Head, face, and eye movements
2. Posture
3. Body position and interpersonal distance
4. Hand gestures
5. Voice quality and tone
6. Personal appearance
7. Use of time

5

Enhancing Personal Magnetism Through Flattery

Call it graciousness, charm, politeness, good human relations, positive reinforcement, office politics, obsequiousness, making others feel good, or sucking up—whatever the name, magnetic people do it consistently. A notable characteristic of personally magnetic people is their ability and willingness to flatter others. If you can learn to flatter others effectively, you will substantially augment your ability to attract and retain supporters.

Flattery works well with about 95 percent of the people who have sufficient mental ability to comprehend the compliments. The young, the old, the rich, the poor, the famous, the unknown, the sick, and the well all respond to sensible flattery. The other 5 percent are people with low self-esteem, the calloused, and the jaundiced. The people who do not respond to flattery ward off compliments, preferring to let their good deeds speak for themselves.

Considering the importance of the topic, I will first speculate why flattery works so well and then present a number of suggestions for making your flattery effective. A striking advantage of learning to flatter is that flattery is a powerful vehicle for enhancing magnetism. Also, learning how to flatter is easier than developing other habits required for being magnetic, such as modifying your thinking patterns or increasing your emotional expressiveness.

Why Flattery Works

An important early step in becoming an effective flatterer is to understand why flattery helps you establish better relationships with others. The root cause of the power of flattery gets at a basic principle of human behavior: People crave being appreciated. The vast majority of people from varying cultures desire recognition. In Asian cultures the desire for group recognition is generally stronger than the desire for individual recognition. Nevertheless, the need for recognition is present.

Much has been made of the contention that the joy of work itself is more important than external recognition, including flattery. The joy of work (or intrinsic motivation) may be a powerful motivator, but even those who get the biggest kick from their work—such as scientists, visual artists, and photographers—crave flattery and recognition. Otherwise they wouldn't compete for Nobel prizes or enter their work in important exhibitions.

Another reason flattery is so effective relates to the normal need to be recognized. Despite all that has been written and preached about positive reinforcement and stroking, most people receive precious little positive feedback. Flattering a person who has not received a compliment in a long time is as powerful as giving a glass of water to a person dehydrated from the sun. Many people hardly ever receive compliments either on the job or at home, thus intensifying their demand for flattery.

Oddly enough, influential people may be more recognition-deprived than less influential people. This is because many people are hesitant to offer a compliment to those in power for fear of being accused of playing office politics or being sycophantic.

The insecurity that many people feel contributes to the effectiveness of flattery. These people would like to think they are doing their job well, being a good family person, or making a contribution in community service. Yet they are not sure, and because of this less-than-complete confidence in the value of their contribution, they welcome external validation. Flatter a person with lurking insecurity and you have drawn that person toward you. Can you remember a time when you felt insecure while performing a new job? How did you feel when someone whose opinion you respected said, "You're doing a great job"?

Flattery is also effective because many people expect charming and tactful people to flatter. If you withhold all flattery, you run the risk of not being perceived as charming and tactful. Given that charm and tact contribute to magnetism, people are more likely to perceive you as magnetic if you flatter them.

Assume that you are still skeptical about the reasons I have given for the importance of flattery. Look at the issue from another perspective: To not flatter others can be a serious career drawback. You can lose out in competition with those who combine good job performance with the ability to flatter. One study on how advancement was achieved at the top levels in major business corporations concluded that a company's top workers tend to be equal in performance. So advancing was based 30 percent on image and 50 percent on face-to-face contacts with the boss. Flattery enters the picture because it can play a big part in enhancing one's image and in contacts with one's superiors.

Psychology professor Roland L. DeLuga studied the relationships between 150 pairs of workers and their managers. His results suggested that from a statistical point of view, flattering the boss added 5 percent to how well the worker was liked and accepted.[1]

John Sabini, chairman of the psychology department at the University of Pennsylvania, offers a cautionary tale about avoiding flattery. He was acquainted with a colleague who was determined not to be labeled a flatterer or a kiss-up. The man landed a coveted teaching and research position at Johns Hopkins University. There he bent over backwards to be rude and insulting. His candor and insensitivity apparently contributed to the young professor's not receiving tenure at Johns Hopkins.[2]

Guidelines for Effective Flattery

Reflect back on the times when you have attempted to flatter someone, or when others have attempted to flatter you. Some of the flattery attempts were probably successful, and in other instances they may have had a neutral or negative impact. The underlying message is that being an effective flatterer requires skill that sometimes transcends common sense.

To help you sharpen your skills in flattering others—and therefore becoming more personally magnetic—I have assembled all the valid information I could find on effective flattery. Somehow, relatively few people have conducted formal research on flattery. Furthermore, more mundane subjects like exploring life on Mars tend to garner more government funding.

To help sensitize you to the importance of flattering effectively, take the accompanying quiz. Even if flattering others is not part of your current repertoire, the quiz might pique your curiosity.

The Flattery Quiz

Answer the following multiple-choice questions. If you have not had an experience similar to the one described in a given question, imagine how you would respond if placed in that situation.

1. A co-worker informs you that he has just won a $5,000 suggestion award from the company. You say to him:
   a. "Congratulations. Five thousand dollars is a lot of money."
   b. "Wow, I wish I were as lucky as you."
   c. "Congratulations. You must be very creative to have won such an outstanding reward."
   d. "I'm so excited for you. I know how I feel when I win something big."
2. A computer operator works for a company that has just merged with another company, making it the largest firm in its field. The computer operator meets the CEO in an elevator. Wanting to flatter the CEO, the computer operator says to her:
   a. "Great job. I knew a bright person like you could pull off the deal."
   b. "Congratulations and best wishes. We are all proud to be working for a company that is the biggest in its field."
   c. "Fabulous job. Can we expect to see you on the cover of *Fortune* or *Business Week* real soon?"
   d. "Good job. The merger is your best accomplishment since you were appointed CEO."
3. A co-worker you do not know well comes to the office with a new hairdo, which you think is quite attractive. You say to her:
   a. "What a stylish new hairdo. You look great."
   b. "I like your new hairdo. It's a big improvement."
   c. "Since when did home permanents come back in style?" [*said with a laugh and smile*].

   d. "That's a wonderful new hairdo. You don't look nearly as old as you did."
4. You are the department manager. One of the group members has just achieved a breakthrough in reducing the time required to complete an important work process. You say to him:
   a. "Great job. Keep up the good work."
   b. "Thank you for a good job. You have now convinced me that you can think creatively."
   c. "Excellent work. You have achieved a top-priority goal for our department."
   d. "Excellent work. What you have done shows that your recent training in reengineering is paying off."
5. You spot Melody, one of the new customer service representatives, walking in from the parking lot. You want to flatter Melody in order to cultivate a good relationship with her, so you say:
   a. "Hi Melody. You look sexy today."
   b. "Hi Melody. I imagine you're one of our best new service reps."
   c. "Hi Melody. You're such a nice person that I would like to take you to lunch soon."
   d. "Hi Melody. Larry [*one of the senior customer service representatives*] told me the other day that you are doing an outstanding job of processing complaints."

Scoring and Analysis: For this quiz, an analysis of the effectiveness of the answers is more important than your total score.

Question 1:

a. Your form of congratulations is too bland. You are complimenting the size of the award more than the person.
b. A terrible compliment. It is not flattering to attribute a person's good fortune to luck.
c. This response is the best flattery technique of the four. You have complimented the person's creative problem-solving ability, thereby pointing to a laudable skill the person possesses.
d. Not a good response. You have made the mistake of talking as much about yourself as about the other person.

Question 2:

a. Not a good response. Flattery directed upward has to be done carefully. As a person of lower status in the organization, you are not in a position to make this kind of evaluation of the CEO's capability.

b. An excellent response because it reflects a sincere form of flattery, and you are not putting yourself in a position to evaluate the ability of the CEO.
c. Not a good response. By setting such high standards for the person you are flattering, you are devaluing her accomplishment.
d. A poor response. You are being presumptuous by evaluating the CEO's performance.

Question 3:

a. A good response. You have complimented her sense of style and her appearance.
b. A poor form of flattery because you have implied that her previous hairdo was a dud.
c. A poor form of flattery because backward compliments are thinly disguised hostility.
d. Another poor response because your compliment will be discounted by its being combined with an insult about her looking old previously.

Question 4:

a. Not a bad response, but too general to be an effective form of flattery. Your response might sound like an overused compliment.
b. Not a very good response because you have combined an attempt at flattery with a negative evaluation of the person's past creative problem-solving ability.
c. An outstanding form of flattery. You have focused in on an important, tangible accomplishment.
d. A mediocre piece of flattery. You are complimenting the training program in reengineering as much as you are the person.

Question 5:

a. Not a good form of flattery, particularly in a work environment. Also, you probably don't know whether Melody wants to project a sexy image on the job.
b. Not a good form of flattery, because you are merely imagining that Melody is effective. Where is your evidence?
c. A poor response. How do you know that Melody would be flattered to have lunch with you?

d. An excellent form of flattery. Mentioning a compliment given by a third party carries substantial weight.

The analysis of responses to the quiz on flattery has hinted at the guidelines and principles of flattery to be described next. Given that effective flattery is a major technique of magnetic individuals, some basic details about flattery are worth your attention.

Use Sensible Flattery

A major guideline for effective flattery is to do it sensibly. As reported in a management newsletter, "There is virtually no limit to the amount of praise that most people can swallow, provided that a spoonful of credibility is added."[3] Credibility in flattery generally refers to saying something positive about the person that is quite plausible. For example, it might be more plausible to say to a date, "You are a great kisser" than to say, "That's the best kiss I've ever had."

Credibility is also increased when you point to a person's tangible accomplishment. A management trainee at a Hewlett-Packard factory told the purchasing manager that she was impressed with his modern operation. "It's quite similar to the ideal materials management system described in my production and operations management course," said the trainee. Her flattery pointed to a tangible accomplishment—the development of a state-of-the art purchasing unit. Her flattery appeared to be instrumental in her being asked to become a permanent member of the purchasing department after her training period ended.

Individualize Your Compliments

A powerful way of using compliments is to individualize them rather than using the same old compliment for everybody. Your work associates will perceive you as insincere if they all hear the same compliments from you. If you intend to use flattery among a group of people who are in frequent contact with each other, maintain a written record of the compliments you have paid to each one. (If the people you compliment have limited contact with each other, there is less danger of your developing a reputation for repeating the same piece of flattery.) This will help you to individualize your compliments, thus adding to their credibility.

An assist toward individualizing compliments is to carefully research what others have done that merits flattery. One man who has been president of two universities practices this technique with aplomb. He carefully scans lists of faculty members' accomplishments and newspaper clippings dealing with faculty research. When he meets a faculty member who has accomplished something notable, the president compliments the faculty member by pointing to something quite tangible. For example, "I see that *Newsweek* quoted you on the validity of supply-side economics. That's great for you and for the school." The president's focused compliments contribute to his magnetism.

Compliment What Is of Greatest Importance to the Flattery Target

Another basic technique in flattering people is to compliment them for their accomplishments in areas of real importance to them. To implement this basic principle, you must first uncover what is truly important to your target of flattery (as suggested in the university president anecdote). Uncovering areas of importance is most cost-effective when your target is someone you intend to flatter several times or more. It is impractical to conduct research on people you will be flattering only once.

Consider the following three methods for uncovering areas of importance to your flattery targets. You might also want to combine one or more of them.

1. *Observe what kind of memorabilia the person keeps in his or her work area.* Professional achievement awards could signify that the person would be most interested in being flattered about work accomplishments. Considerable space devoted to family photographs could signify that your flattery would be best aimed at your target's personal life. Considerable space devoted to sports and hobbies, such as bowling trophies or team photos, would suggest another area for flattery.

2. *Observe carefully what your target talks about with the most enthusiasm.* If the person is preoccupied with work and profes-

sional accomplishments, focus your compliments and other forms of flattery on those areas. If, on the other hand, your target appears preoccupied with family life and recreation, use those as subjects for flattery.

3. *Send out a trial balloon when first flattering someone.* Offer a small dose of flattery directed toward work. If your target comes to attention quickly, you have probably touched the right button. If you get a very small reaction, switch to flattery in another area. In many instances, it may make the most sense to return later with another flattery attempt.

To illustrate the above point, here is an example of flattery that had a negative effect on its target.

> A research scientist who was very proud of his pioneering work on optic fibers took a position as a senior scientist at an IBM research laboratory. Wanting to ingratiate himself with the scientist, a neighbor engaged him in conversation during a barbecue. The neighbor complimented the researcher on working for such a great company, and went on at length about the magnificence of Big Blue. The scientist quickly became bored and excused himself by saying that his piece of chicken cooking on the grill was now ready.
>
> The well-intentioned neighbor did not realize that the scientist was a proud individual who much preferred to be complimented on his work in optic fibers. He was not moved by compliments about IBM despite his positive attitudes toward the company.

Flatter Others by Listening Intently

Paying people compliments is a major, but not the only, technique of flattery. Listening intently to another person is also a powerful form of flattery. The technical term for listening intently is *active listening*. It refers to listening for the full meaning of what someone is saying without making premature judgments or interpretations. The person who is the recipient of active listening feels important and is likely to attribute many positive qualities to the listener. Just as most people do not receive enough compliments, most people also suffer from not being listened to enough.

Listening as a form of flattery will not work well unless your target person senses that you are listening. Consider these approaches to listening intently and communicating the fact that you are listening:

- *While your target is talking, look at him or her intently.* At the same time, maintain a steady eye contact. Such concentration on your target will be much appreciated.
- *Hold your fire.* A common barrier to effective listening is the habit of mentally preparing an answer while another person is speaking. The fact that you patiently wait your turn to speak is an extraverbal sign of good listening.
- *Nod your head in agreement from time to time.*
- *Mutter "mmh" or "uh-huh" periodically but not incessantly.*
- *Ask open-ended questions to encourage the other person to talk.* For example, you might ask, "What do you think of our company's subcontracting manufacturing to companies that use political prisoners as part of their workforce?" Your target will then be encouraged to express his or her opinion. A close-ended question covering the same issue would be: "Do you think it is ethical for our company to subcontract manufacturing . . . ?" Your target can readily answer yes or no to the second question, which allows little room for much listening. (Of course, asking the target's yes or no opinion is still a small form of flattery.)
- *Reflect your target's content or meaning.* An effective way of reflecting meaning is to rephrase and summarize concisely what the group member is saying. In response to the above question, your target might have said: "What a horrible thing. Good heavens, when I think of those poor prisoners working away like slaves for pennies a day, it makes me sick. That's worse than sweatshops." You might respond, "You are concerned about the human rights issues in using prison labor." Feeling understood and listened to, your target might say: "That's exactly what I mean. I'm glad you understand my position."
- *Reflect the other person's feelings.* This is sometimes even more effective than reflecting content or meaning. Reflection-of-feeling responses typically begin with "You feel that. . . ." In the above

interchange, you might say, "You feel quite upset that our company is subcontracting to companies that rely on the labor of political prisoners." Feeling understood, your target might feel drawn to you, giving you an element of magnetism.

- *Interpreting what is happening is another approach to active listening.* The interpretation is designed to give the person being listened to insight into the nature of the problem. (In this situation, your flattery target is somebody over whom you have formal responsibility.) For instance, a store manager might be listening to the problems of a department manager with regard to the cleanliness of his work area. After a while, the store manager might say, "You're angry and upset with your employees because they don't keep a careful eye on housekeeping. So you avoid dealing with them, and it only makes matters worse."
- *Keep your ratio of talking to listening down to about 1 to 5.* In other words, spend 20 percent of your time talking, and 80 percent listening. Most nonmagnetic people reverse the ratio.
- *Ask yourself if anything the other person is saying could benefit you.* Maintaining this perspective will enable you to benefit from most listening episodes, and will motivate you to listen intently.

Flatter by Referring to or Quoting the Person

Your acute listening skills have prepared you to implement another hard-hitting tactic for flattering others. The tactic spins off from the adage, "The sincerest form of flattery is imitation." By referring to or quoting (including paraphrasing) another person, you are paying that person a substantial compliment. If you don't listen carefully to people, you will not be able to quote them or refer to what they have said or done.

Part of the technique in question is to make reference to how your target handled a given situation. You might say, for example, "When Ashley faced a similar crisis, here's how she worked her way out of it." Referring to a person or restating his or her thoughts has many positive connotations:

- You think what the person does is important.
- You think what he or she has to say is important.

- You are proud to quote the person because his or her thoughts make you look good.
- You identify with the person.
- You are making a public statement that you think what your target says or does is important.
- You think the person makes a good role model.
- You like the person.

Referring to what another person has said is flattering whether or not your restatement is accurate. Most people will object to a complete misrepresentation of their comments but forgive a slight inaccuracy. Another consideration is that most people are so pleased when their name is mentioned (such as at a meeting) that they neglect to ask for details about what was said. The accuracy of your reference to what another person said is therefore likely to go unchallenged.

Referring to and quoting another person has two important links to personal magnetism. The people you refer to and quote will be drawn to you, thus increasing your base of those who regard you as magnetic. Since personal magnetism is based to a large extent on what other people think of you, the larger your number of fans the more magnetic you are in reality.

The second link to magnetism is that the ability to acknowledge the contributions of other is a behavior found among many magnetic and charismatic people. Personally magnetic individuals are usually gracious in sharing credit. They are secure enough to recognize that many of their accomplishments reflect the contributions of others.

A case in point is Rick Pitino, the popular basketball coach who is also in demand as a motivational speaker for business firms. When Pitino is interviewed about winning an important game or having a successful season, he typically deflects comments about his extraordinary coaching skills. Instead, he talks about the outstanding efforts of his players and other members of the coaching staff. Acknowledging the contributions of others is a wonderful way of projecting magnetism.

Use Confirmation Behaviors

A general approach to making others feel good is to use confirmation. The term refers to a series of behaviors that have a positive or therapeutic effect on other people. A confirmation behavior on your part adds to the feelings of self-worth enjoyed by the receiver of your words or actions.

Since confirmation behaviors have such a positive effect on others, they are likely to be perceived as a form of flattery. The risk in using confirmation behaviors to flatter others is quite small. If a statement you make to another person is not perceived as flattery, using confirmation behaviors still adds to your magnetism.

Praise is a natural confirmation behavior and can be considered another form of giving a compliment. The person who is praised is likely to feel important and needed. Praise is usually considered the responsibility of a manager, but co-workers can also dispense praise. Phil Tyler, a magnetic marketing consultant, makes praise part of his regular routine. His praise is effective because it zeroes in on specific behavior. Phil can praise even when he disagrees with a person's position.

Phil was present at a tense meeting in which several different points of view were expressed. After the meeting, Phil said to Shirley, one of the participants: "Shirley, I want to thank you for expressing your well-reasoned opinion. It doesn't matter that you and I disagreed. We are not going to solve problems unless we have enough courage to bring forth different opinions."

Courtesy is another important confirming behavior. When an outsider visits an organization, he or she typically receives the most courteous treatment from the most powerful and influential people. For example, a CEO will typically greet an outsider by using the person's last name, while lower-ranking people generally opt for the first name. The point is that influential people—many of whom are magnetic—think courtesy is important. Acts of courtesy that others might consider a form of flattery include:

- *Asking a visitor if he or she would like to use the phone.*
- *Treating the lowest-ranking employee with respect.* You might, for example, ask permission of a custodial worker to walk across a freshly mopped floor.
- *Responding promptly to e-mail inquiries and letters.*
- *Promptly returning telephone calls.*
- *Not keeping a visitor waiting for more than five minutes.*
- *Taking the initiative to open the door when walking with another person of either sex.*

• *Writing notes of appreciation to people who have extended themselves for you.* A surprisingly large proportion of successful people send notes of appreciation to lower-ranking people. Steve Ross, the late chairman and chief co-executive of Time Warner Inc., was highly regarded for his memos of appreciation, which he signed "Love, Steve." Many magnetic people handwrite notes of appreciation to add a touch of warmth (and to avoid the suspicion of having sent a form letter).

• *Acknowledging the presence of other people.* As basic as this simple human relations technique may appear, it is often neglected. Your courtesy will therefore be noticed if you do not allow the presence of others to go unnoticed. Even a simple "Hello" to a person of modest position in the organization will be perceived as courteous.

• *Offering an explanation for your actions.* Explaining why you need something in a hurry or why you want a certain task performed enhances your stature as a courteous person. A manager might say to a graphic designer, for example, "I know my time demands are difficult. Yet if you can get this design done by Friday, we can make the deadline for the Chicago trade show." Offering this explanation for the request is also effective because the manager thereby shows that he respects the graphic designer's time.

• *Avoiding abrasiveness.* In today's highly competitive workplace, abrasiveness toward work associates appears to be on the upswing. Despite a generally healthy economy, many workers fear losing their job and not being able to find suitable replacements. This job insecurity often translates into abrupt and abrasive treatment of others in order to get one's ends accomplished. As one manager told a staffer who wanted to leave early to attend his daughter's soccer game: "I don't care if your daughter's playing in the World Cup. Leave early today and you may find your desk emptied out tomorrow." Being abrasive is not only unflattering; it also detracts from magnetism.

Acceptance of others is another powerful confirming behavior. Accepting another person doesn't mean that you necessarily like everything the other person does, but it does show that you are not being judgmental. Acceptance is closely tied to valuing cultural diversity. A notable act of acceptance took place at a telecommunications company during the year-end holiday season. Ted, the president, was strolling down the hall. He ran into Jerry, an information systems specialist, who made no particular attempt to hide his sexual orientation (gay) when talking about his private life. Ted said to Jerry, "If you are planning to come to the holiday party, don't neglect to invite your partner." Score one for being tolerant, accepting, valuing diversity, and magnetic.

Two other key confirming behaviors are giving compliments and actively listening, both of which have already been described. The message is the same. Compliments and active listening enhance the feelings of self-worth in others. The feelings of self-worth, in turn, add to your stature as a magnetic person because you made somebody else feel better.

Give Positive Feedback

A mild form of flattering others is to give them positive feedback about their statements, actions, and results. Technically speaking, compliments are an extreme form of positive feedback. I refer, however, to flattering people by giving them a straightforward declaration of what they did right. Positive feedback might also be considered a confirming behavior because it adds to the self-worth of others. The ability and willingness to give positive feedback contributes to magnetism because people are drawn closer to those people who deliver such feedback. Here are three suggestions for giving positive feedback:

1. *Make the feedback specific.* Pinpoint what the person did right by saying something on this order: "Your suggestion for using smaller boxes for mailing our products resulted in a $90,000 savings the first year." Specific feedback is more motivational than a general statement such as "Thanks for the great suggestion."

2. *Provide some of your feedback in public.* The most widely accepted adage in human relations is "Criticize in private, praise in public." When in a group setting, most people glow when you point to a specific contribution they have made. Using the above example, you would say, "Bill's suggestion for using smaller boxes. . . ."

3. *Provide the feedback close in time to the good deed.* A basic principle of positive reinforcement is that the reward should follow close in time to the behavior that merited the reward. Recognizing that you might have a busy, cramped schedule yourself, set a realistic goal of providing positive feedback (even a one-minute message) within five working days of the good deed you want to recognize. The Internet is becoming an excellent vehicle for sending positive feedback while you are on a business trip. However, the burden is on you to carry along people's Internet addresses. Or maybe you are good at memorizing these addresses. If so, the next section of this chapter will be easy.

Remember Names

A final suggestion for flattering others is to remember the names of people with whom you have infrequent contact. (It's hardly flattering to remember the name of a close work associate.) Remembering the names of people upon first meeting them is reasonably impressive; it allows you to use their names when saying goodbye. Even more impressive is remembering names when meeting people for a second or third time.

Remembering the names of people is flattering because it makes them feel important. Charismatic leaders have a superb ability to remember names, or perhaps they develop this skill only after becoming leaders. Whatever the truth is, people in high-level positions have a much better-than-average ability to remember the first and last names of people they see only infrequently.

Although elaborate systems have been developed to help you remember names, practicing a few basic guidelines will suffice for developing this important skill. Included are two suggestions to help you avoid embarrassment when a person's name does not come to mind.

- *Take a risk on seeing whether you know a person's name.* Most people who complain about their inability to remember names play it safe by not addressing casual acquaintances by name. Suppose seated next to you at a meeting is somebody you were introduced to three weeks ago. You think you know the person's name, but you are not sure. Take a chance by saying, "I remember you well. Let me see if I have your name correct.'' Being right is a confidence builder. Being wrong is not so bad. At least you are magnetic enough to try to remember.

• *Upon first meeting, carefully listen to the person's name and then repeat it several times.* Tell the person you want to make sure you have heard the name correctly, or are pronouncing it right. For example, ''Am I correctly pronouncing Sumantra Ghoshal?'' And, of course, when the meeting ends say, ''See you again, Sumantra.''

• *Concentrate carefully when you first hear the name.* No magical memory system can exempt you from the fact that remembering names requires concentrated listening.

• *Study the person's name tag or security badge when they are worn.* However, if you are nearsighted, it might look a bit suspicious if you move your head within six inches of the person's tag or badge.

• *Ask for the person's business card, then study the name immediately and associate it with the person's face.*

• *When convenient and sensible, use a word association.* Make an association between the person's name and physical appearance if a good fit comes to mind. If you meet a person with the first name Molly, you might think of a molecule dancing over her head. Or if you meet a person with the last name Davenport, think of him sitting on a sofa. When you really have to stretch, forget the association. It will be too far-fetched to remember. Or maybe you are good at making a visual association with Sumantra Ghoshal that you will remember.

• *If you forget a person's name, and don't want to admit it, play for time.* Say to the person, ''Could you please refresh my memory on the correct pronunciation (or spelling) of your name?'' Of course, if the person has a name like Ann Jones, your ploy will probably be transparent.

• *If you are missing a name when you want to make an introduction, allow for a self-introduction.* Suppose you are talking to one person, and another person joins you whose name you have learned but cannot recall. Ask, ''Have you two met?'' Most of the time they will introduce themselves, getting you off the hook.

A reader of your mental caliber hardly needs a review of enhancing magnetism through flattery, but for the record, I first described why flattery works. Above all, people want to be appreciated. The basic guidelines for effective flattery are as follows:

1. Use sensible flattery.
2. Individualize your compliments.
3. Flatter others by listening intently.
4. Flatter by referring to or quoting the person.
5. Use confirmation behaviors (such as praise and courtesy).
6. Give positive feedback.
7. Remember names.

6

Charismatic Qualities You Can Develop

So far, you have read about many of the characteristics, actions, and attitudes of personally magnetic people. To assist you in further understanding magnetism, and in enhancing your own magnetism, it is also important to study qualities associated with charisma. My emphasis is on charismatic qualities that are capable of development, at least to some extent. The information presented earlier about thinking patterns and emotional expressiveness would also apply to charismatic people.

With self-discipline and practice, you can take on many of the traits, characteristics, and actions of charismatic people. Assume that a person is an ultraconservative decision maker. With a goal in mind, that person can prod himself or herself to engage in some of the risk taking typical of charismatic people.

Before delving into the twelve charismatic qualities that are capable of development, let's first try to understand what *charisma* means. For our purposes it is a type of charm combined with other special qualities that inspire others. Yet charisma has also been defined in many other ways. A sampling of these definitions will help you to understand why developing your charisma can have such a big impact on your career and personal life. Representative definitions of charisma are as follows:

- A divinely inspired gift (from its Greek origins).
- A special quality of leaders whose purposes, powers, and extraordinary determination differentiate them from others.

- Endowment with the gift of divine grace.
- Leadership that has a magnetic effect on people.
- The process of influencing major changes in the attitudes of people and of building their commitment to the goals of the organization.

Although charisma is closely tied to leadership, people can be charismatic without holding a leadership position. Visualize for a moment a charismatic athlete, actor or actress, newscaster, professor, teacher, physician, or nurse. All of these people can influence others without occupying a formal leadership position. Their ability to influence others lies in their personal characteristics.

By developing or adopting some of the traits, characteristics, and behaviors of charismatic people, you can demystify charisma. Although some facets of charisma can be attributed to having an inspired gift, many aspects of it can be developed. If you accept the assumption that components of charisma can be developed, you move charisma (and magnetism) away from the mystical realm.

Develop Self-Confidence

Self-confidence is important for charisma as well as for exercising leadership. Self-confidence is important because it helps assure the people you are attempting to influence that things are under control. If people look to you for direction, they want you to behave in a confident, assured manner. Yet if you are too arrogant about things, they may lose that sense of assurance.

Diane Harris, a former vice president in charge of acquisitions for Bausch and Lomb Inc. is now the principal in her own consulting firm. Harris has earned a national reputation as a business strategy specialist, and is well respected by her colleagues. While in her corporate position, Harris would occasionally get outsiders to talk about professional matters. When making the contact, Harris did not allude to her prestigious position. She would simply mention her company and department. Despite her prestige and power, Harris is modest and gracious. She appears quite confident, but in an easy, nonpompous way. Harris's behavior is representative of many charismatic people.

Self-confidence is generally achieved by succeeding in a variety of situations. A confident sales representative may not be generally self-confident unless he or she also achieves success in activities such as taking exams, navigating the Internet, writing good memos, and displaying athletic skills.

The technique of using positive self-talk, described in Chapter 2, is a useful confidence builder. Let's explore three other specific strategies for building and elevating self-confidence. They will generally work unless the person has deep-rooted feelings of inferiority.

Inventory Your Personal Assets and Accomplishments

Many people suffer from low self-confidence because they do not appreciate their own good points. Therefore, a starting point in increasing your self-confidence is to take an inventory of your personal assets and accomplishments. Personal assets should be related to characteristics and behaviors rather than to the tangible assets, such as real estate, you may own. Try not to be modest in preparing your list of assets and accomplishments. You are looking for any confidence builder you can find.

Asking others close to you to provide input for your list is a useful supplement. For many people, positive feedback from others does more for building self-confidence than does feedback from oneself. The reason is that self-esteem depends to a large extent on what we think others think about us. Consequently, if other people whose judgment you trust think highly of you, your self-image will be positive.

The value of these asset lists is that they add to your self-appreciation. Most people who lay out their good points on paper or in a computer file come away from the activity with at least a temporary boost in self-confidence. The temporary boost, combined with a few success experiences, may lead to a long-term gain in self-confidence.

Develop a Solid Knowledge Base

An essential for projecting self-confidence is the development of a base of knowledge that enables you to provide sensible alternative solutions to problems. Intuition is very important, but working from a base of facts helps you to project a confident image. Formal education is an obvious and important source of information for your knowledge base. The day-by-day absorption of information directly and indirectly related to your career is equally important.

Use Positive Visual Imagery

Assume you have in mind a situation in which you would like to appear confident and in control. An example would be a meeting with a major customer who has told you over the telephone that he is considering switching suppliers. Your intuitive reaction is that you cannot handle his objections without fumbling or appearing desperate and that you will probably lose the account. An important technique in this situation is *positive visual imagery*, or picturing a positive outcome in your mind.

To apply this technique in this situation, imagine yourself engaged in a convincing argument with your customer aimed at his retaining you as his primary supplier. Imagine yourself talking in positive terms about the good service your company offers and how you can rectify any problems. Visualize yourself listening patiently to your customer's concerns and then talking confidently about how your company can handle these concerns. As you rehearse this moment of truth, create a mental picture of you and the customer shaking hands over the fact that the account is still yours.

Positive visual imagery helps you to appear self-confident because your mental rehearsal of the situation has helped you prepare for battle. If imagery works for you once, you will be even more effective in subsequent uses of the technique.

Develop Your Ability to Create Visions

The term *vision* is now routinely mentioned in reference to corporate and political leaders. An effective leader is supposed to have a vision, whereas an ineffective leader lacks one. The idea of a vision is closely linked to charisma. Charismatic people inspire others with their vision, or an idealized version of what an organization or organizational unit can become. You can also have a vision for your investment club, your place of worship, your neighborhood, or a local athletic team.

If you can create visions for others, it will be a major force in your being perceived as charismatic. To form a vision, one has to look beyond the immediate future to create an image of what the organization or unit is capable of becoming. A vision is designed to close the discrepancy between present conditions and ideal conditions. The vision thus goes beyond present realities.

A vision uplifts and attracts others. An example is the vision created by Craig McCaw, who sold the firm he founded (McCaw Cellular Communications) to AT&T. While in the cellular business, he created a vision of it as the growth engine of the telecom industry. Later, he conceived an entirely new way to deliver the Internet by creating a constellation of 840 satellites. The system would be able to transmit signals from any point on the planet to any other with the speed and capacity of fiber-optic cable. A key part of the vision is that the Internet would be possible without being dependent on wires.

Attesting to McCaw's charisma, Bill Gates invested $10 million of his own money in McCaw's new venture, Teledesic. Gates said, "I wouldn't have invested in Teledesic unless Craig was involved. He is an amazing person. Craig thinks ahead of the pack and understands the communications business and where it is going better than anyone I know."[1]

People like to listen to the spinner of visions, yet a vision needs some plausibility to capture people's attention. To create a vision, obtain as much information from as many of the following sources as necessary:

- Use your own intuition about developments in your field, the markets you serve, demographic trends in your region, and the preferences of your constituents.
- Study the work of futurists (specialists in making predictions about the future) as it relates to your type of work.
- Hold a group discussion of what it would take to delight the people your group serves.
- Scan annual reports, management books, and business magazines to uncover the type of vision statements being formulated by others.

- Speak to group members and friends individually and collectively to learn of their hopes and dreams for the future. Uncover their values and aspirations.
- If you are formulating a vision for an organizational unit, study the organization's vision. You might get some ideas for matching your unit's vision with that of the larger organization.

Whether or not you are a manager, describe your vision from time to time. Share your work-related vision with your co-workers, manager, and customers. Share your personal life vision with friends and family members. Creating a vision for your family will add to your charisma at home.

If you are wondering what a vision statement actually sounds and reads like, look at these two examples—one corporate and the other from the field of community sports:

1. *CNN:* To create the first truly global information company, the global network of record, seen in every nation on the planet, and broadcast in most major languages.
2. *Gremlins (a Little League soccer team):* To create a soccer team that is the envy of the city because of the way in which we develop the body, minds, and good citizenship of children between 5 and 8. Winning will only be a byproduct of having fun and giving every team member an opportunity to participate.

Be Enthusiastic, Optimistic, and Energetic

A major behavior pattern of charismatic people is their combination of enthusiasm, optimism, and high energy. Without having a high standing on all three characteristics a person is unlikely to be perceived as charismatic by many people.

A remarkable quality of charismatic people is that unlike most others, they maintain high enthusiasm, optimism, and energy throughout their entire workday and beyond. An executive search consultant (headhunter) based in New York City made this comment about the strongest prospects he pursues:

> I've had meetings as late as 10 at night with the executives I'm pursuing. They are as fresh as if it were 8:30 in the morning. You'll never hear one of them complain about how late it is or that he or she is exhausted. When these managers talk about their jobs or careers, they have a gleam in their eyes.

Al Dietzel, the head of financial and public relations for The Limited in Columbus, Ohio, is an extreme example of the high-energy profile of charismatic people. He trained for six months in a gym to prepare for the celebration of his sixty-fifth birthday. The events of that day, starting at 7:15 A.M., followed this sequence: a ninety-minute tennis match, losing to his daughter, age 41 →yoga stretching →a 155-pound bench press →a two-mile run around the athletic club with his nineteen-year-old grandson, in eighteen minutes, three seconds →a tandem jump out of a Cessna at 10,000 feet →eighteen holes of golf, with a score of 93 →shower →dinner with his family.[2]

One might argue that Dietzel was just pulling a dramatic stunt. Nevertheless, he had to be optimistic, enthusiastic, and energetic to execute the feat. You can develop your enthusiasm and optimism by searching for the positive elements in a given situation. Elevating your energy level takes considerable work, but here are few feasible suggestions:

- *Get ample rest at night, and sneak in a fifteen-minute nap during the day when possible.* If you have a dinner meeting at which you want to shine, take a shower and nap before the meeting.
- *Exercise every day for at least ten minutes, including walking.* Allow no excuses such as being too busy or too tired, or the weather being bad.
- *Switch to a healthy, energy-building diet.*
- *As a long shot, experiment with over-the-counter energy enhancers that include a dose of iron.*
- *Keep chopping away at your To Do list so that you do not have unfinished tasks, draining away your mental energy.*
- *Attempt to get your personal problems under control so that they do not drain your productive energy from work.* Similarly, get your

work problems under control so that they do not drain energy from your personal life.

Another aspect of being enthusiastic, optimistic, and energetic is to have an *action orientation.* The term refers to wanting to get things accomplished and decisions implemented. "Let's do it" is the watchword of the charismatic person. An action orientation also means that the charismatic person prefers not to agonize over dozens of facts and nuances before making a decision. After collecting enough information to reinforce intuition, the charismatic person takes action and encourages others to do the same.

Be Sensibly Persistent

Closely related to the high-energy level of charismatics is their almost-never-accept-no attitude. I emphasize the word *almost* because outstanding leaders and individual contributors know when to cut their losses. If an idea or a product simply won't work, the sensible charismatic absorbs the loss and moves on in another more profitable direction.

An executive at a telecommunications company said:

> A test of executive material in our company is whether the middle manager has the guts to kill a failed project. Some managers become so ego-involved in a product they sponsored, they fight to keep it alive long after it should have died. They twist and distort financial information to prove that there is still life left in their pet product. A person with executive potential knows when to fold his or her tent.

Jack Canfield, a motivational speaker and entrepreneur, offers this sound advice: "Persevere and you will succeed. The secret to persevering is building your self-esteem so you can take rejection and move on to the next opportunity. Self-esteem is critical. I'm living proof of the idea's validity."

The living proof Canfield offers is that thirty publishers rejected his manuscript for *Chicken Soup for the Soul*. Canfield and his co-

> author finally attended a booksellers' convention and sold the book to a small publisher, Health Communications. Ultimately the book became an extraordinary best-seller and was followed by a best-selling sequel. At last report, Canfield, his co-author, and staff were sharing royalties on 7 million books. The success of his books also led to an extraordinary surge in Canfield's speaking and seminar business.[3]

A person can develop persistence by the simple expedient of acting like a persistent person. Knock on a few more doors, hunt for one more alternative solution to a problem, and encourage others to do the same.

Be Candid

Charismatic people, especially effective leaders and managers, are remarkably candid and open with people. Although not necessarily insensitive, the charismatic person is typically explicit in giving his or her assessment of a situation. When asked to give an employment reference for a student whose performance and behavior she did not think highly of, a charismatic professor said: "If you want a positive reference, find another professor who has a higher evaluation of your work. In the classes you took with me, you did not show the kind of work that makes for a successful employee." The student was shocked and disappointed at first, but learned an important lesson. He was jolted into realizing that how he performed today influenced his opportunities tomorrow.

Charismatic people are candid on the positive as well as the negative side. They size up people and situations quickly and accurately and are willing to share their perceptions. Charismatic people speak directly rather than indirectly so that people know just where they stand. Instead of asking a worker, "Are you terribly busy this afternoon?" the charismatic leader will say, "I need your help this afternoon. Are you available?" Expressing thoughts directly parallels expressing feelings directly, as explained in Chapter 3.

Becoming candid is not easy if you have acquired long-term habits of circumlocution and a diplomatic softening of your thoughts. An important goal in being candid is that the people with whom you interact should have no doubt about your true opinion. Just before expressing your opinion about a person, idea, or object, prepare a statement of about ten words in your mind. Done frequently, this activity will build your skill in expressing thoughts candidly. Here are six examples of candid expressions relative to work and personal life:

- "You are definitely promotable."
- "Your job will be terminated in thirty days."
- "You are an outstanding performer."
- "I would like a committed relationship with you."
- "I care for you, but marriage is not a possibility."
- "Sorry, I choose not to golf with you any longer."

For the person learning to be candid, the initial results are likely to be a pleasant surprise. Quite often the recipient of the candid expression will say something to the effect, "Thanks for being honest. I'm glad I know where I stand." A charismatic person's success in being candid is partially attributable to the way in which the message is delivered. A negative message is most likely to be accepted when it is delivered in a matter-of-fact, nonjudgmental, nonretaliatory, and nonhostile manner.

Promote Yourself

Charismatic people look out for number one. Self-promotion is an important part of their repertoire. Instead of being concerned about appearing arrogant, charismatic people look for opportunities to let others know of their talents and capabilities. Many charismatic people in high places hire publicists to keep the media aware of their new ventures and other accomplishments. A world-class example is Richard Branson, chairman of Virgin Enterprises, a $2 billion conglomerate heavily involved in entertainment and consumer products.

Branson is well known around the world and rivals members of the royal family for recognition in his home country, England. His reputation as an "adventure capitalist" has placed him in the spotlight as a glamour boy who mingles with the jet set. Virgin's holdings now include a gigantic retail store in Times Square in New York City. Branson boldly predicts that Virgin soft drinks will soon rival Coca-Cola and Pepsi in worldwide sales.

Branson's self-promotions were instrumental in launching his enterprise. From his perspective a photo or an article about him was free advertising, made much more effective if he was speed-boating across the Atlantic or hot-air ballooning from Japan to the Canadian Arctic. Risking his life was part of running a business.

Few aspiring charismatics can be as swashbuckling as, or have the financial resources of, Richard Branson. Yet most people can implement a handful of self-promotional tactics. Consider several of these possibilities, or use them to spark ideas of your own.

- *Create your own World Wide Web page touting your accomplishments.* Put your Web address on your business cards and stationery.
- *Have a business card developed and printed with your résumé on the back.* (Yes, it can be done and it is impressive to some people.) Freely hand out your card.
- *Establish a personal accomplishment file containing every letter, memo, or report that specifies your contribution.* Objective information, such as cost savings achieved by your idea, is much better than an opinion about your contribution. Display your file when your performance is being reviewed or you are under consideration for a transfer, promotion, or special assignment.
- *Establish a diary of special projects.* The diary, or work journal, might take the form of a daily or weekly listing of the nonroutine work you do. Provide extra details on all the big problems you tackle. Use this file for the same purposes as you use your accomplishment file.
- *When speaking to work associates or people outside of work, casually mention any exciting project you might be working on.*
- *Be a name dropper.* Let others know of influential people who have visited your office or home or with whom you have played tennis or golf.
- *Hire a publicist for even a few hours per month to help get your name dropped in the right places.* A woman in Buffalo, New York,

paid a publicist to obtain publicity for her maternity clothes store. Now the owner is regularly quoted in the business section of her local newspaper whenever an article appears about local entrepreneurs. The publicist accomplished the initial job in just four hours of consultation.

Take Sensible Risks

Charismatic people not only have an action orientation; they are also willing to take sensible risks. The term *sensible* refers to situations in which the risk taker believes that he or she has enough skills to control the uncertainties in that situation. To reflect on your own propensity for taking risks, do the accompanying exercise.

What Is Your Propensity for Risk Taking?

Indicate how well each of the following statements reflects your attitudes or behavior, using the following scale: very inaccurately (**VI**); inaccurately (**I**); moderately well (**MW**); accurately (**A**); very accurately (**VA**). Circle the number under the category that best fits.

	VI	I	MW	A	VA
1. If I had a serious illness, I would purchase generic instead of brand-name drugs.	1	2	3	4	5
2. I invest (or would invest) much more money in bonds or CDs (certificates of deposit) than in stocks.	5	4	3	2	1
3. The thought of starting my own business appeals to me.	1	2	3	4	5
4. I am (or was) willing to go on blind dates frequently.	1	2	3	4	5
5. My career advice to young people is to pursue a well-established occupation with a high demand for newcomers to the field.	5	4	3	2	1

	VI	I	MW	A	VA
6. I would be willing to relocate to a city where I had no family or friends.	1	2	3	4	5
7. During the last few years, I have taken up a new sport, dance, or foreign language on my own.	1	2	3	4	5
8. My preference is to have at least 90 percent of my compensation based on a guaranteed salary.	5	4	3	2	1
9. From time to time I buy jewelry, clothing, or food from street vendors.	1	2	3	4	5
10. The idea of piloting my own single-engine plane over the ocean appeals to me.	1	2	3	4	5

Score ______

Scoring and Interpretation: Obtain your score by adding the numbers you have circled.

46–50 You are a heavy risk taker, bordering on reckless at times. Your tendency to take risks that are too high might detract from your charisma.

38–45 You probably are seen as a sensible risk taker and as an adventuresome person in a way that enhances your charisma.

10–37 You have a propensity to avoid risks. Your conservatism in this regard could detract from your charisma.

We have all heard of entrepreneurs who started businesses by borrowing money on their credit cards and from friends and by taking out a second mortgage. Although this would seem to be an outlandishly high risk to the outsider, the entrepreneur feels sufficiently in control to proceed. Jack Canfield of *Chicken Soup* fame had $48,000 in credit card debt when he invested time and money in attempting to sell his book. Canfield says he knew *Chicken Soup* was best-seller material, so he invested his time and some money in getting it published.

Being convinced that sensible risk taking is associated with charisma is not sufficient to make you more charismatic. Others must also be aware of your risk taking so that it has an impact on their perception of you. You would have to make your risk taking visible to people you want to influence. Talk widely about the sensible risks you have taken and explain the results you achieved.

There is another way to benefit from the link between risk taking and charisma. As you become comfortable taking risks, you will gradually develop a more adventuresome personality. Since an adventuresome personality is part of charisma and magnetism, you will have developed in the right direction.

Be Extravagant and Flamboyant

Extravagance and flamboyance are characteristic of many, but certainly not all, charismatic people. The person who spends far more money than others would for goods or services that serve the same or similar function will capture attention. Letting others know that you smoke $25 cigars will make you charismatic to some, yet annoy and irritate others. A comparable act of extravagance and flamboyance is to have your favorite snack food or restaurant meal sent by overnight express from a distant city. Many will be impressed, but others will look askance at your conspicuous consumption.

Tom Monaghan, the founder of Domino's Pizza, is perceived as charismatic by many people. His passion for buying things added to his mystique. At one time he spent $150 million for a half-mile-long building to serve as company headquarters in Ann Arbor, Michigan. He embellished the surrounding farmland with a petting zoo and herds of cows and buffalo. The headquarters building contained a $40 million collection of Frank Lloyd Wright artifacts. Headquarters also included a two-story personal office suite with silk ceilings and leather floor tiles. Monaghan's extravagance and flamboyance were also displayed in his purchase of the Detroit Tigers baseball team and an island in Lake Huron.

Later, when his company faced severe financial pressures, Monaghan did a 180-degree turn, and led an austere life for a CEO and founder of a national company.[4] Nevertheless, his earlier extravagance contributed to his charisma.

Given that extravagance costs so much money, most people

need to invest their charisma dollars selectively. If you are unable or unwilling to buy a professional sports team or a $40 million art collection, be creative in making smaller purchases that contribute to extravagance and flamboyance. For example, you might talk a lot about your $25 cigars but smoke only two or three per year. A few moderate-cost extravagances for your consideration include:

- Take a vacation in Iceland and bring back photos.
- Purchase a simulated elegant sports car in which a fiberglass body is placed on the chassis of an ordinary vehicle. You can hear the oohs and ahhs as you cruise into the company parking lot with a 1936 Mercedes roadster.
- Buy a simulated railroad watch circa 1910 for $60 because the authentic ones sell for about $6,500. Use the watch in a business meeting.
- Flash a $150 fountain pen since most of your colleagues are more likely to have writing instruments worth only a tenth that amount.

Have an Attention-Getting Pastime

Closely related to being extravagant is having an attention-getting pastime because many of these activities require extravagance. An example of this principle in practice is Steven R. Appelton, the chairman and CEO of Micron Technology Inc. One of Appelton's pastimes is remaining in superb physical condition. His weight training and disciplined food habits enable him to maintain 5 percent body fat. Appelton also skydives, competes in the triathlon, motorcycle races, and collects and flies airplanes, including an A–37B Dragonfly.[5]

Another highly placed charismatic executive is Chrysler Corporation President Robert A. Lutz. Although he occupies the number-two executive position in his company, Bob Lutz is revered by many in the auto industry. He is thought to have been passed over for the top job because of his political clashes in the past with Lee Iacocca. Lutz flies a jet plane and is often photographed at the controls, dressed in jet-fighter gear.

As with being extravagant, financial constraints help determine the nature of one's attention-getting hobby. Apply your creative problem-solving ability to finding an attention-getting (and rewarding) pastime. Ann White, a colorful personality and one-time bar owner, gained considerable attention via a once-a-year event she staged. Each Thanksgiving she opened her house and offered a free meal to any needy person or family. Although White was never deluged with visitors, her gesture received a good deal of publicity that added to her allure.

Other low-budget, attention-getting pastimes include learning Star Trek language (yes, they have a language of their own), rescuing stray pets with injuries, being a street counselor to the disadvantaged, and sending friends limericks you write about them.

Be Humanistic

A comprehensive characteristic of many charismatic people is their humanism. *Humanistic* is a catchall term that refers to almost any appeal to the emotions and feelings of others. An especially important part of humanism is showing concern for both the work and personal lives of others. If you express an interest in the total individual and his or her multiple roles in life, you are being humanistic. It is easier to display humanism on the job when you are a manager.

The perception of you as being charismatic will increase when you behave humanistically. Leaders with a high standing on charisma are often those with a reputation for the kindness and warmth they extend to their constituents. Sam Walton, a charismatic leader, was often lauded for the kindness he displayed toward Wal-Mart employees. Many employees looked upon "Mr. Sam" as a father figure who had their best interests in mind.

Here is a list of twelve humanistically oriented attitudes and actions you can take on in relation to group members.

1. *If you are the manager, initiate a "dress down" day.* This would encourage employees to dress in the type of casual clothing they ordinarily wear while running or doing household chores.

2. *Buy a baby gift for a new parent's child.*

3. *Ask group members about their career and life style aspirations.* Ask how well their jobs are fitting into their career plans and what hopes they have for future jobs.

4. *Ask group members what you can do to make their jobs easier.*

5. *Conduct a group meeting to discuss all the company programs that could possibly make life easier for employees, such as dependent-care assistance.*

6. *Grant an employee an afternoon off from work to invest in any activity that will make life easier.*

7. *Conduct a luncheon discussion about the major sources of stress on the job and what can be done about them.*

8. *Write personal notes at mid-year to high-contributing group members.* Express appreciation for their help in keeping the organization operating and also mention how they make life easier for you.

9. *Give employees proper credit for any of their ideas that you use.* A major employee complaint is that managers use their ideas without giving appropriate credit.

10. *Invest at least a couple of hours per month in listening to the personal problems and complaints of employees.* Let them give vent to their confusion and anger, but avoid becoming their counselor. If an employee's problem appears to be overwhelming, suggest that he or she visit the employee assistance program or seek outside help.

11. *Ask in a friendly, noninquisitive way about the physical health of group members.* Ask about what the person is doing for physical exercise.

12. *Ask about the health, happiness, and major activities of family members.*

If you can implement most of these suggestions, your reputation as a humanistic and charismatic manager will be enhanced. Furthermore, you will have displayed an advanced knowledge of human relations on the job.

Display an In-Your-Face Attitude

In general, the preferred route to being perceived as charismatic is to be positive, warm, and humanistic. Yet some people earn their charismatic reputation through toughness and nastiness. An in-your-face attitude may bring you some devoted supporters, but it will also bring you many detractors. The tough attitude is attractive to people who themselves would like to be mean and aggressive.

> A dramatic example of a charismatic leader with an in-your-face attitude is Scott Paper Co. Chairman Al Dunlap. He earned the nickname "Chainsaw Al" during his two-year stint with the company. Dunlap transformed Scott from a poorly performing company to a huge profit maker. Under his leadership, company stock surged 225 percent, and earnings also reached record heights. To accomplish these financial feats, Dunlap eliminated 11,000 jobs and raised prices.
>
> At other companies too, Dunlap has displayed an in-your-face attitude. A boxer during his days at West Point, Dunlap attacks and challenges nearly every premise and person in sight. He dismisses as rubbish the idea that a company has an obligation to groups other than its stockholders. With a satisfied grin over his accomplishments at Scott, he awaited his next assignment at a company that needed to be "Dunlapped." His next assignment proved to be the turning around of Sunbeam Corporation.[6]

An in-your-face attitude can create fear in others, assuming that you are in a position of power. Too much combativeness on the way up will often lead to an early career demise. Turnaround managers like Dunlap may be charismatic, but many of them employ bodyguards. The negative, abrasive approach is a much longer shot than the more positive strategies and tactics that have been described.

Be Dramatic and Unique

A final strategy for becoming more charismatic is really an amalgam of the ideas already introduced. Being dramatic and unique in significant, positive ways is a major contributor to charisma, which in turn enhances your personal magnetism. Being dramatic and unique stems from a combination of factors such as being energetic, promoting yourself, taking risks, demonstrating extravagance, and showing extra care and concern for others. When feasible and sensible, stand out by being unique. Marlene Caroselli, a consultant in leadership and language, tells this anecdote about a person who enlivens others with his uniqueness:

> A young man in a Fortune 500 firm was asked by his boss to give a presentation on time management to his peers. To illustrate the point that we need to have schedules and adhere to them, he deliberately entered the conference room five minutes late. He rushed in wearing a jogging suit and running shoes and apologized while peeling off his "sweats" to reveal his business suit underneath. Upon conclusion of his speech—to make his point all over again—he flew out of the conference room, pulling on his jogging outfit as he ran, and breathlessly explaining that he was late for another meeting.[7]

In this chapter I have described twelve important characteristics, behaviors, and attitudes that contribute to charisma. In quick review, they are as follows:

1. Develop self-confidence.
2. Develop your ability to create visions.
3. Be enthusiastic, optimistic, and energetic.
4. Be sensibly persistent.
5. Be candid.
6. Promote yourself.
7. Take sensible risks.
8. Be extravagant and flamboyant.
9. Have an attention-getting pastime.
10. Be humanistic.
11. Display an in-your-face attitude.
12. Be dramatic and unique.

7

Specific Bonding Actions and Attitudes

To better understand magnetism and to become more personally magnetic, you need to consider yet another perspective. Magnetic people form bonds between themselves and others. The same can be said for charismatic leaders, who often form bonds with their constituents.

The bond between the magnetic individual and the target person does not have to be a long-term one. Quite often the magnetic individual forms a relationship that might last only a few days, an hour, or even less. Bonding situations can arise when someone is making a sale, convincing higher management during a budget negotiation, or receiving a lesser penalty from a judge for a traffic violation. A magnetic person can also form quick relationships at social functions, such as engaging a stranger in conversation.

The purpose of this chapter is to describe certain actions and attitudes you can use to help you form both short-term and longer-term bonds with people. The fact that you form these bonds makes you magnetic. Many people will argue for the reverse: Because you are magnetic, you can form bonds with people. From a skill-development perspective, however, one must start somewhere. If you engage in the behaviors characteristic of magnetic people, you will be perceived as magnetic.

Discover the Needs and Motivators of Others

A starting point in forming a bond with another person is to find an answer to the question: "Why would this person want to form a bond with me?" The question will help you uncover how your influence target will benefit from a brief or longer association with you. If you know why someone might benefit from a relationship with you, it is possible to indicate the promise of offering those benefits. The analysis of two different scenarios will illustrate how this approach might work.

Scenario 1: A New Co-Worker Arrives

Connie, a research analyst, works at a large financial services firm. She wants to increase the number of her allies and supporters in the office. Connie also has a genuine interest in being helpful to others. One day Connie is introduced to Jeannine, a research analyst who will be joining the team. Jeannine appears to be in her mid-twenties, makes an excellent professional appearance, and has an MBA from a leading business school.

Connie would like to be helpful to Jeannine, and she would also like to enlist her as an ally. Connie reasons that other team members probably have similar motives. So Connie decides to take a tactical approach. She asks herself several questions:

- What kind of help might Jeannine need?
- What can I offer Jeannine that could be useful?
- What actions should I avoid that might irritate Jeannine?

Connie listens intently to Jeannine during a get-acquainted luncheon arranged by the team leader. She hears Jeannine talk about the challenge she is facing in being in a new city away from friends and family. Connie also hears Jeannine refer to the fact that she is looking forward to being able to devote so much energy to her job now that she is no longer working on her MBA. Jeannine appears to be technically competent and confident about her ability to perform well.

After the luncheon, Connie mentions briefly to Jeannine that she would be glad to help her get adjusted to the company and to the city, but does not offer specifics. She listens intently when Jeannine says with a smile, "Jasper—he's my cat—and I have a lot to learn about this city. Without friends and family in town, it's a slow start."

Connie's quick analysis is that Jeannine places a high priority on friends, family, and home life. Even the mention of her cat could point in that direction. The next day, Connie drops by Jeannine's cubicle, and says, "I have two things that might be of interest to you. First, here is my vet's card. He not only specializes in cats, he loves them. I'm sure Japser will be very pleased. He might be due for his leukemia shots." Jeannine laughs, at the same time expressing appreciation and delight.

With her first attempt at friendship working so well, Connie is encouraged to continue. "Here's what else I have in mind," says Connie. "My family and I are having a cookout at my house late this Sunday afternoon. We want you as our honored guest." (Notice the effectiveness of a late Sunday afternoon invitation. It is much less disruptive to plans than other possible times such as Saturday night or early Sunday afternoon.) Jeannine graciously accepts the offer, has a wonderful time, and quickly befriends Connie.

The vet and cookout offers were not random attempts at friendship. Connie correctly observed that Jeannine was placing high priority on domestic-type activities in getting established in town. If Connie had observed that Jeannine was more interested in meeting prospective dates, she would have invited her to join her at a happy hour event geared toward meeting singles.

Scenario 2: The Older Worker

Jeff is the newly appointed supervisor of a customer service department responsible for filling telephone orders for machine parts. Jeff sincerely wants to be an effective leader of the department. To do so he must form a good relationship with each member of the department. One of Jeff's influence targets is Ralph, a worker in his mid-sixties, which makes him older than Jeff's father.

Jeff suggests that he and Ralph have a get-acquainted session, something he is doing with all other group members. One of the questions Jeff asks during the meeting is how well satisfied Ralph is with the company and the job. Ralph responds that everything is fine.

"I'm glad to know that things are *fine,*" Jeff remarks. "My concern is what could be done to convert your job into an *outstanding* experience." Ralph responds cautiously, "Some people around here don't think I learn as fast as they do. You know how it is. Many young people have a negative stereotype about a person with gray hair."

"We have no room for negative stereotypes in this department," replies Jeff. "I think with your vast knowledge of our customer requirements, it would be easy for you to apply new techniques to our business."

Ralph looked pleased but still somewhat skeptical. So Jeff decides to execute a bonding action based on Ralph's concerns about negative perceptions of his learning ability. "I have an assignment that I would like you to handle for the department," continues Jeff. "I want you to be our department representative at a seminar on using the Internet to improve parts distribution. Your assignment is to bring us back information to make us more productive."

"Very thoughtful of you to ask," responds Ralph. "I'm fascinated by the Internet, and I welcome the opportunity to apply my knowledge further."

Jeff has formed a bond with Ralph that can serve as the start of an excellent working relationship. Jeff uncovered Ralph's concern about being perceived as a slow learner because of his age. He then assuaged that concern by giving Ralph an assignment that required good learning ability.

Be a Nurturing, Positive Person

A humanistic approach to bonding with others is to be a nurturing, positive person. A nurturing person promotes the growth of others. Magnetic people are often nurturing, but so are many kind and considerate people who are not particularly magnetic. Nurturing people are positive and supportive, and typically look for good qualities in others. A toxic person stands in contrast to a nurturing person because he or she dwells on the negative.[1] Visualize the following scenario to appreciate the difference between a nurturing person and a toxic one.

> Jason, an accountant, enters the office where two co-workers are talking. One is a nurturing person, the other is toxic. With a look of con-

cern, Jason says, "I'm sorry to barge in like this, but can anybody help me? I've been trying to send a fax to Singapore. The fax machine is caught in the redial mode. I know from experience that the phone company treats each redial like another call. We could be running up hundreds of dollars in long-distance charges for this one call. I've punched the stop button but the machine keeps redialing."

Janet, the nurturing person, says, "I'm not a fax machine expert, but since I'm not the one with the jammed fax message, I can be calm enough to help." Alex, the toxic person, whispers to Janet, "Tell Jason to pull out the fax manual. If you help him now, you'll only find him on your doorstep every time he needs help."

If you listen to toxic people long enough, you are likely to feel listless, depressed, and drained. Toxic people have been described as energy vampires because they suck all the energy out of you. Nurturing people, by contrast, are positive, enthusiastic, and supportive. These behaviors add to their magnetism.

A mental attitude that fosters nurturance is recognizing that most people have a need for self-fulfillment, although people vary widely in the extent of this need. You might engage in interactions with co-workers and subordinates such as sharing new skills with them, clipping relevant news articles, or telling them about an important new on-line file you have discovered. You might also advise them of a book or seminar geared to their professional interests.

Being a nurturing, positive person is a lifelong process rather than a tactic to be used at will. Nevertheless, making a conscious attempt to be nurturing and positive can help you develop the right mind-set. Take the following quiz to give you some preliminary insights into your willingness to help others in your work environment.

My Attitudes Toward Helping Others

Describe to what extent you agree with the following statements by using a three-point scale: disagree (**D**); neutral (**N**); agree (**A**). Circle one of the choices for each question.

1. If I see a co-worker make a mistake, I do not inform him or her of the mistake. D N A

2. It should be part of everybody's job to share skills and ideas with co-workers. D N A
3. The manager should have exclusive responsibility for coaching people within the work unit. D N A
4. I can think of many instances in my life when somebody thanked me for showing him or her how to do something. D N A
5. I have very little patience with co-workers who do not give me their full cooperation. D N A
6. To save time, I will do a task for another person rather than spend my time showing him or her how to do it. D N A
7. I would take the initiative to put an inexperienced worker under my wing. D N A
8. As a child, I often took the time to show younger children how to do things. D N A
9. Rather than ask a co-worker for help, I wait until the manager is available to help me. D N A
10. It is best not to share key information with a co-worker because that person could then perform as well as or better than I do. D N A

Score ______

Scoring and Interpretation: Use the following scoring key to obtain your score for each answer, and then calculate your total score.

1. D = 3, N = 2, A = 1
2. D = 1, N = 2, A = 3
3. D = 3, N = 2, A = 1
4. D = 1, N = 2, A = 3
5. D = 3, N = 2, A = 1
6. D = 3, N = 2, A = 1
7. D = 1, N = 2, A = 3
8. D = 1, N = 2, A = 3
9. D = 3, N = 2, A = 1
10. D = 3, N = 2, A = 1

25–30 If you scored in this range, you have very positive attitudes toward helping, developing, and training others in the workplace. Such attitudes reflect a compassion for the growth needs of others and strong teamwork.

16–24 You have mixed positive and negative attitudes toward helping, developing, and training others in the workplace. You may need to develop greater sensitivity to the growth needs of others to be considered a strong helper of others and a good team player.

10–15 You have negative attitudes toward helping, developing, and training others in the workplace. You should guard against being so self-centered that it will be held against you.

Be a Mentor

A standard way of helping others—being a mentor—can also be instumental in forming bonds. Being a mentor alone will not make you personally magnetic, but it contributes to others perceiving you as warm and helpful. Mentoring a person of lower rank is a familiar practice, but a newer trend is to mentor a co-worker. There are many different roles a mentor plays. As you study the mentoring roles listed, search for several that would fit your style or capabilities. Offer to be somebody's mentor, and use several of these roles as ways in which you might help your protégé.

- *Be a sponsor by nominating your protégé for a promotion or desirable assignment.*
- *Coach your protégé by giving that person on-the-spot advice on improving job skills.* Being a coach is an excellent way of being perceived as magnetic.
- *Protect your protégé from potentially harmful situations or from the boss.* For example, the mentor might tell her protégé, "In your meeting today with the boss, make sure you are well prepared and have all your facts on hand. He is in an ugly mood and will attack any weakness."
- *Give challenging assignments to your protégé and then provide feedback.* If you are a co-worker, perhaps you can request that your protégé help you with a difficult task.
- *Be a role model by giving your protégé a pattern of values and behaviors to emulate.* Projecting such values can make you an inspiring individual.

• *Be supportive and encouraging just by way of being accepting.* An outstanding characteristic of magnetic people is their acceptance of others.

• *Be a counselor to your protégé by listening to his or her problems and then offering advice.*

• *Be a trusted friend to your protégé. Trust* in this context means that the mentor does not pass on confidential information about the protégé or engage in back-stabbing.

• *Encourage your protégé to solve problems on his own and to make his own discoveries.* A comment frequently made to mentors is "I'm glad you made me think through the problems myself. You jogged my mind."

Recognize the Human Spirit

A soft and fuzzy, yet powerful, approach to bonding with others is to recognize the human spirit. By *human spirit,* I mean the human and emotional aspects of an undertaking. In a quest for efficiency, it is easy to dismiss the relevance of certain rituals that in reality contribute to motivation and productivity. To an efficiency-minded person, the laughing and warm-up that take place during the early stages of a meeting may seem like a waste of time. The Type A person might say to himself or herself, "Why are these people wasting so much time? If we got on with the task, we could finish the meeting early and move on to other work."

The efficiency-minded person is certainly right that much time wasting takes place during a meeting when people chat and laugh about extraneous matters. (Such warm-up activity can also be found outside of meetings.) Yet the camaraderie may actually be contributing to team spirit and, therefore, to productivity.

The personally magnetic individual creates a bond with others by recognizing the importance of the human spirit in most work endeavors. This is the reason that charismatic leaders so often favor work celebrations, parties, and companywide town meetings. They want to appeal to the human spirit even though it is difficult to identify a direct link between the human spirit and productivity. Here are some specific ways in which you can recognize the human spirit and in this way foster a bond between yourself and your influence targets:

- Hold a celebration after an important milestone is reached such as making the first shipment of a new product.
- Put a ''Welcome Back'' sign and balloons over the desk of an employee returning from maternity or paternity leave.
- Hold a brief grieving session for victims of downsizing.
- Get the entire department together on a Saturday afternoon to help rehabilitate the flood-damaged house of an employee who did not carry flood insurance.
- Devote an hour of a staff meeting to discussing how company values influence work on a day-by-day basis.
- Celebrate diversity by displaying flags representing the native country of each worker in the department.

Engaging in too many activities of this sort could of course be hokey. Yet the magnetic individual conducts just enough of them to arouse the human spirit. Arousing the human spirit is an effective vehicle for creating bonds between yourself and the people you want to influence.

Demonstrate Concern for Others

Showing concern for others, whether you are a manager or an individual contributor, helps form bonds. Concern for others might also be seen as another manifestation of humanism. Managers have a concern for others when they do not look upon people as machines or software that are readily replaceable or interchangeable. A manager or leader who forms bonds with group members is sincerely and deeply concerned about their welfare.

A leader who is heavily involved in the welfare of group members will, when possible, put the interests of group members first. For example, the manager might come to the office during her vacation to straighten out a payroll problem. Concern of this type helps build loyalty. And loyalty functions as a bond between group members and the leader.

How do platitudes about concern for others mesh with the

requirement that one part of a manager's job is to take decisive action against laggards and other poor performers? The following information contributed by consultant Gerald Graham illuminates this issue:

> A manager admitted that he had an employee who was performing poorly. "He has not been performing well for some time. I've counseled him several times. I think he's had some personal problems. I suggested that he visit our Employee Assistance Program counselor. He wouldn't even consider that."
>
> The manager offered many reasons for, in his words, "not wanting to run the employee off": There was a lot of training invested in him. It was hard to hire good replacements. He had been with the company five years. He was in an important position. He needed the job. It was really hard to terminate a person.
>
> Graham explains that there are unseen consequences when managers do not make the tough calls (in this case, disciplining and perhaps termination). Like some varmints, these unseen consequences have a way of wiggling into the deep grass before we can spot them. Even the manager with the highest concern for people must ask critical questions about the consequences of retaining a poor performer:
>
> - What opportunities are lost?
> - How much does the inept employee hinder overall performance?
> - How many customers are not served well?
> - How much is lost in revenues that would otherwise have been available for investment and new development?

A scenario relevant to this issue took place in a small office. Two key employees were clearly not meeting their responsibilities, but the manager failed to act, saying "I don't want to see them lose their jobs." However, the two had such a negative impact on revenues that executives at headquarters closed the branch, thereby putting fifteen people out of work.[2] A manager with a better-reasoned concern for human welfare might have dealt squarely with the two poor performers. Doing so could have presented fifteen people from losing their jobs.

If the constructive action taken with the poor performer helps the employee to get back on track, it may create a bond between the manager and the poor performer. Many poor performers in fact recognize that they are headed down the road to a career crisis. The poor performer who rebounds with the manager's help will form a bond with that manager, which is fueled by appreciation.

Win the Respect of Others

Another tough-minded way of forming bonds with others, and of contributing to your personal magnetism, is to win their respect. Showing concern for others, as just described, is one strategy for winning the respect of others. Another key strategy is to demonstrate that you are capable of handling a difficult task related to your expertise. If you perform the task under extreme pressure, so much the better for your reputation.

> Gregory Brenneman, the thirty-something chief operating officer of Continental Airlines, provides a superb example of creating a bond by winning the respect of others. Brenneman combines outstanding human relations skills with a keen analytical mind for solving business problems. Before being invited to join the company, Brenneman worked for Continental as a consultant. He impressed top management by helping the airline lower its maintenance costs from $777 million to $500 million. The simple expedient of moving the maintenance operation out of Los Angeles, with its high overhead costs, resulted in an annual savings of $65 million.
>
> Later, as a company executive, Brenneman gained the respect of top management and many employees with his rigorous analysis of the importance of training airline reservations attendants. His analysis revealed that trained attendants generated $22 per sales call, versus $14 for those who were untrained. He pointed out that training takes only five hours, yet a former executive in a cost-cutting blitz eliminated the training. Brenneman reinstalled the training. He comments, "I love making a difference, and doing it quickly."[3]
>
> Brenneman has a loyal following at Continental. Part of his appeal is the contrast between him and Continental founder and former hatchet man and CEO Frank Lorenzo. The combination of Brenneman's people skills and impressive analytical feats contributes substantially to the bonds he has created between himself and Continental personnel.

Paula Cholmondeley is another example of how gaining the respect of people can create bonds. She holds the dual job titles of Corporate VP, Owens Corning, and President, Miraflex Fiber Products. She has earned considerable respect from those in her work environment, partly because of her winning risk-taking style. Miraflex is an Owens Corning business unit that developed its product, a new type of fiberglass, in conditions of top secrecy. Under Cholmondeley's leadership, the factory to produce the fiberglass was built within an unusually tight time frame.

"I had to learn to operate at a new level of risk," says Cholmondeley. "Sometimes we ordered costly equipment after just one trial." All the speed and hush-hushness of the operation paid huge dividends for the company and her career. Cholmondeley helped reduce the time it usually takes to move an invention from the idea stage to a customer-ready product from four years to two. Owens Corning was able to slip Miraflex onto retailers' shelves in record time, thus surprising the competition.[4]

As is true of all effective leaders, Cholmondeley's accomplishments were a team effort. Yet her ability to spearhead the effort to develop a major new product under heavy time pressures won her enormous respect. In the process, Cholmondeley bonded with people and enhanced her magnetism.

Use a Memorable Handshake

For a moment, let's switch from an emphasis on mental attitudes and skills to an everyday physical action. Another contributor to forming bonds with people is your handshake. Yet few people give much thought to their handshake other than to follow the basic principle of making it firm. I include several ideas from negotiation specialist Roger Dawson in my suggestions for using your handshake as a bonding device. Dawson believes strongly that the right handshake adds to charisma.[5]

- *Begin by getting feedback on your handshake.* Ask about six people, including work associates, friends, and family members, to rate your handshake on a 1-to-10 scale. Demand specifics as to what they like and don't like about your handshake. One person who asked for feedback found out that people who wore several rings did not like his handshake. His handshake was forceful enough to press the rings into the other person's flesh thus producing a cutting sensation.

• *If you have a weak or limp handshake, exercise regularly to strengthen your grip.* Use a spring grip exerciser or squeeze a tennis ball daily.

• *As you shake hands, gaze carefully enough into the other person's eyes to note their color.* Observing the color will establish a twinkle in your eye and also create a brief interaction between you and that person.

• *If you are a man shaking hands with a woman, kiss the top of her hand.* For extra panache, say *enchanté* (the French word for enchanted or charmed) as you kiss her hand. You will be remembered for your charm and old-fashioned gallantry.

• *At the moment of shaking hands, think a very positive thought about the other person.* The positive thought will help you to project warmth and acceptance.

• *If you are attempting to shake hands with a person whose hand is deformed, do not hesitate to give the person a full handshake.* People with deformed hands are accustomed to hesitancy and awkwardness on the part of others. If you can overcome this physical bias, you will have made good progress toward forming a bond.

• *If you intend to shake hands with a person who lacks a right arm, shake his or her left hand.* Although in our culture the right hand is used for shaking, it is much more courteous to shake the left hand than to omit the gesture altogether.

• *If you have only a left hand or left arm, use it for shaking rather than miss out on an opportunity for bonding.* Observe how Senator Robert Dole, the Republican presidential candidate in 1996, shakes hands. His right arm is nonfunctional so he shakes with his left.

• *Shake with a dry and clean hand.* A wet hand, or one sticky with food, creates an extremely negative impression.

A sensational handshake alone will not make you magnetic and charismatic or create strong bonds with others. Combined with other techniques, however, it will be a big contributor.

Build a Personal Relationship With Your Influence Target

Mutually rewarding working relationships often lead to personal relationships, such as co-workers as well as managers and group members becoming friends outside of work. The work relationship becomes the starting point for establishing a bond between two people. At times you can reverse this process to your advantage. You first build a relationship with the person outside of work, then use it as a bridge for building a work-related bond with your influence target.

An application of this tactic would be to focus on a person in the office with whom, so far, you have only a neutral relationship. Your goal is to cultivate this person so that you form at least a reasonable bond on the job. So you invite this person to a party at your house or to an athletic event.

At this point you may be saying to yourself, "So what's new? Getting to know a work associate socially in order to build a better working relationship is a standard technique." You are eminently correct, except that you may not have anticipated the punch line. The skilled bond-building, magnetic person practices this tactic gingerly. Off the job, do not try to win points about work-related matters. In the midst of a conversation at your house, do not say, "Incidentally, I need a more rapid turnaround from you in getting your input for my project."

Keep the social roles and work roles separate. If the personal relationship with your target develops well, it should spill over naturally to the job. A skillful office politician never plants a work harpoon during off-hours. Instead, he or she focuses on building a climate of acceptance that will lead to a stronger bond and more cooperation in the office.

Respond Positively to Criticism

A masterful technique for creating bonds with people—and incidentally demonstrating class—is to respond positively to criticism. Being able to accept and profit from criticism has a shock value because so few people have the ego strength to do so. Most people become defensive and retaliatory when criticized. But if you respond positively to criticism, you may create a bond with the criticizer. At the same time, you will add an element of magnetism to your style. Here are several suggestions for dealing with criticism, including two methods that will often get the other party on your side.[6]

See Yourself From a Distance

Place an imaginary Plexiglas shield between you and the person giving the criticism. Attempt to be a detached observer looking for useful information. Assume a professional, problem-solving point of view. Ask yourself, "What is this person telling me that will help me perform my job better or get along better with him (or her)?" At the same time, attempt to depersonalize the situation. Act as if an automotive technician were giving you advice on what must be done to enable your car to pass inspection. Would you take it personally if you were told that your struts need to be replaced?

Ask for Clarification and Specifics

Ask politely for more details about the negative behavior in question so that you can change it if change is warranted. If your boss is criticizing you for not having good cultural sensitivity, you might respond: "I certainly do not want to be culturally insensitive. I need your help in working on this problem." After receiving the details, you can better determine if the criticism is valid.

Respond Appropriately to the Critic

An important part of learning from criticism is to respond appropriately to your critic. Let the criticizer know what you agree with. Apologize for the undesirable behavior by saying something like this: "I apologize for not having good cultural sensitivity. I know what I can do differently now. When we entertain visitors from another culture, I will do some research about what actions or saying might offend that group. Don't worry, I'll never put my feet on the desk again when talking to a visitor from the Middle East."

The response with the biggest potential for forming a bond with your critic is to thank him or her. Explain how you have profited from the experience—to wit, "Thank you. I appreciate your help. Becoming more culturally sensitive should help me deal better with employees and customers."

Disarm the Opposition

As an extension of the point just made, you will often decide to agree with the criticizer because this person has a legitimate complaint about your behavior. If you deny the reality of the complaint, he or she will continue to harp on the point and the issue will remain unresolved. An unresolved issue can block the formation of a bond. By agreeing with the criticism, you may set the stage for a true resolution of the problem.

Agreeing with criticism made of you by a superior is effective because by doing so you are then in a position to ask for his or her help in improving the situation. Rational managers realize that it is their responsibility to help group members overcome problems, not merely to criticize them. Imagine that you have been chronically late with reports during the past six months. It is time for a performance review and you know that you will be reprimanded for your tardiness. You also hope that your manager will not downgrade all other aspects of your performance because of your tardy reports. Here is how disarming the opposition would work in this situation:

Your boss: Have a seat. It's time for your performance review, and we have a lot to talk about. I'm concerned about some things.

You: So am I. It appears that I'm having a difficult time getting my reports in on time. I wonder if I'm being a perfectionist. Do you have any suggestions?

Your boss: Well, I like your attitude. Maybe your *are* trying to make your reports too perfect before you turn them in. I think you can improve in getting your reports in on time. Try not to figure everything out to four decimal places. We need thoroughness around here, but we shouldn't overdo it.

Disarming is effective because it takes the wind out of the other person's sails and has a calming effect. The other person is often waiting to clobber you if you deny your guilt. If you admit guilt, you are more difficult to clobber. Admitting to your errors is an admirable quality that will help form a bond between you and your critic.

Invest Time in One-on-One Sessions

A final bonding maneuver to be described here is perhaps the easiest to implement, yet at the same time powerful. If you are a manager, invest time in individual meetings with staffers to discuss their job satisfaction and their aspirations. (The same technique helps communicate your humanism.) Take people who report to you to lunch on a random basis. Avoid selecting only personal favorites or problem people. Not only will these sessions enhance people's perception of you as a magnetic individual, they will create bonds.

If you are not a manager, take the initiative to ask your boss for a ten-minute session just to discuss your situation in the company. Focus on positives, express appreciation, and avoid giving the impression that you have a hidden agenda. Speak directly rather than evasively. To repeat, your best opportunity for bonding takes place within the intimacy of a person-to-person discussion.

In this chapter I have considered a powerful strategy for enhancing magnetism—finding ways to form bonds with others. I have suggested ten techniques that will facilitate bonding with others, as follows:

1. Discover the needs and motivators of others.
2. Be a nurturing, positive person.
3. Be a mentor.
4. Recognize the human spirit.
5. Demonstrate concern for others.
6. Win the respect of others.
7. Use a memorable handshake.
8. Build a personal relationship with your influence target.
9. Respond positively to criticism.
10. Invest time in one-on-one sessions.

8

Using Humor to Exude Magnetism

Humor and magnetism are related in ways that provide a call to action for the person who wants to become more magnetic. Humor acts as a magnet that draws people toward the creator of the humor. Others are naturally attracted to someone who uses humor effectively. Furthermore, we like to be around those who make us feel good, and humor is one of the most powerful feel-good devices there is. People laugh when they feel good, and they feel good when they laugh.

Humor is also important for magnetism because it is a bonding device between you and your influence targets. Robert Orben, the dean of humor experts, once said:

> If you're a leader, you're viewed from a distance by the average person. When you are giving a speech, you are on stage. You don't want this emotional separation from people. Telling them a joke says, "I understand your problems, and I am with you. It's you and me against them." That's the focus of what I have tried to do in the business community for years—show people that, if you can laugh together, you can work together.[1]

One purpose of this chapter is to explain how and why humor is so important for magnetism and charisma. An even more important purpose is to package enough information about the nature of humor so that you can use humor to enhance your magnetism. If you've had a change of mind about becoming more magnetic, there's still no need to skip this chapter. You can use many of the ideas just to be a more entertaining work associate, family member, or friend.

Why Is Humor Funny?

If we asked a six-year-old why humor is funny, the child would most likely respond, "Because it makes you laugh." Suppose you probe further with the question, "Yes, but why does humor make you laugh?" The child would probably respond, "Because it's funny." If we look at a few serious definitions of humor, perhaps we can understand why it is funny and makes us laugh. If you know why humor is funny, it will be easier for you to be humorous in a way that adds to your magnetism.

The key ingredient to a joke, as with any form of humor, is the element of surprise. You take people down one train of thought and then switch to another. John Cleese, a well-known producer of humorous training films, explains that a joke involves a sudden switch from one frame of reference to another. For example:

> A woman conducting a survey into sexual behavior was questioning an airline pilot. She asked him finally, when he had last made love. He replied, "1993." The survey taker was most surprised because pilots have a reputation for being amorous. "1993?" she asked. "Well, it's only 2216 now," he replied.[2]

The sudden shift in frame of reference from a year date to the twenty-four-hour time system is exactly what makes the joke funny. Your mind is jolted in a pleasant, constructive way. Suppose a person is asked, "How can you spot a house in which no teenager lives?" The typical frame of reference would be that the house avoids some negative consequence of having a teenager present.

The person responds, "Oh, I guess the house is much neater or more tranquil." The person who asked the question replies, "Wrong. The numbers 12:00 keep flashing on the VCR." Instead of teenagers being ridiculed, adults are the butt of this joke. The implication is that the teenager has enough high-tech savvy to set the VCR, while the adult lacks such capability.

John Morreall, a philosophy professor, offers more details

about the element of surprise in humor. He says that humor is "the enjoyment of having something out of place, something that violates your expectations, something that doesn't fit your picture of the way things are supposed to be."

Several executives have capitalized on the element of surpise by pulling a similar stunt in recent years. While making a presentation to employees, they suddenly take off their suit jackets. You can see a quizzical look on the faces of many in the audience. Next, the executive opens the front of his shirt to reveal—a T-shirt with the company logo. People attending the meeting shout, rave, and clap.

The enthusiasm generated by shedding two layers of clothing to exhibit a company T-shirt stems from a double surprise. Having a male executive open his shirt is a big surprise; having a female executive do the same is a quadruple surprise. The intensity of the surprise multiplies when the executive reveals a T-shirt with a company logo underneath.

A third theory of why humor is funny, or at least enjoyable, is that humor is primarily an expression of human aggression. We use humor to disparage another group, and then revel in the disparagement. Humor is therefore thought to be beneficial because it is safer to make verbal digs at people than it is to physically attack them. The extremists of this point of view believe that aggressive humor even helps to prevent wars.

Whether or not the humor-as-aggression theory is correct, the magnetic person should minimize or avoid hostile humor. Many magnetic and charmismatic people have the goal of uniting rather than dividing people. They thus avoid hostile jokes such as those that disparage a person's ethnicity, gender, race, age, or physical condition. Most people are aware that such jokes clash with the spirit of diversity and that they have therefore in large part disappeared from the repertoires of managers with modern attitudes.

To avoid appearing too politically correct and straitlaced, I admit that there are times when a skillfully told ethnic joke can unite rather than separate people. Credit venerable comedian Henny Youngman for this joke unifying two ethnic groups:

> Did you hear the one about the American Indian woman who married a Jewish man? They decided to give their new son a name to please both sides of the family. They named him Whitefish.

Less recognized as a form of hostility than ethnic jokes are those that disparage selected occupational or professional groups. A newly appointed president paid an official visit to the company's finance division. Many accountants and a few economists, in addition to finance specialists, were employed by the division.

The purpose of the visit was to conduct an open forum rather than to give a prepared talk. The president began with what he thought was an effective joke. He said, "Do you know what an economist is? He's somebody who was good with numbers in school but didn't have the personality to become an accountant." The president was an economist himself, so he thought that by indirectly poking fun at his profession, his joke would be appreciated all the more.

Nobody laughed, however, and the president's meeting was off to a poor start. With just one brief joke, the president had insulted the interpersonal skills of both economists and accountants. His joke was also a mild putdown of women because economists were depicted as exclusively male. This one-liner fits the aggression theory of humor because an insult is a form of hostility.

A hostile joke or teasing comment is sometimes effective when the insult is of moderate intensity. It also helps when the group being insulted is a rival of the group present. (The economist/accountant joke insulted those present.) Here is a widely circulated aggressive joke that nevertheless adds to the stature of the person who presents it:

Question: "How can you tell when a personal computer belonged to the people in (the rival or disliked group)?"
Answer: "There's a bunch of whiteout on the screen."

The Characteristics of Effective Humor

To improve your chances of using humor successfully to enhance your magnetism, it pays to understand the characteristics and attributes of effective humor. Of particular relevance are the characteristics of effective humor on the job. How well you present a clever comment, including your extraverbal language, is also a fundamental requirement for using humor effectively. Several of the following characteristics stem from an understanding of what makes humor funny. Use these characteristics as a checklist in evaluating whether to use a particular witty comment or joke.

Effective humor is spontaneous.

Making a witty or clever comment on the spur of the moment makes a vastly bigger contribution to personal magnetism than telling rehearsed jokes does. Telling jokes can help you develop a reputation for being funny and a good storyteller. Yet a joke teller is rarely considered witty. The witty comment that follows helped establish the reputation of a product manager at Procter & Gamble. The product manager was walking in downtown Toronto with three work associates. Toronto, like many major cities, has about one beggar holding out a styrofoam cup every ten feet in the retail and entertainment district.

The product manager flipped a two-dollar coin into the cup of a beggar—a healthy-looking man in his mid-forties. One of her work associates asked why she would give money to a healthy-looking beggar. The product manager replied: "I empathize with the guy. If our latest product fails to get the market share we forecast, we'll all be joining him next month."

Effective humor in a work setting avoids insulting those present.

As explained in the comment above about economists and accountants, it is a bad idea to insult the people present. When outside groups are attacked or insulted, the attack should have a soft, human touch. A member of a sales group used this variation on the most widely used joke of the past two decades: "How many marketing specialists does it take to change a light bulb?" Answer: "Three. Two to conduct a nationwide survey of whether changing a light bulb leads to customer delight, and one to make the actual change if needed."

Creative variations on the light bulb joke are effective in part because light bulb jokes are a shared experience. People wait for your spin on changing light bulbs so that they can evaluate your originality. (Did you find the hidden pun?)

Humor that delivers a positive stroke to the audience is particularly effective.

A deeply ingrained behavior pattern of magnetic and charismatic people is to make others feel good through their humorous comments. If this is a skill that has not come naturally, it takes a long time to develop. The starting point is to raise your level of awareness that it is important to build the esteem of others.

Funny comments that enhance the self-esteem of those present typically exaggerate the capabilities of the people involved. The sales director of a company that made car interiors for automotive manufacturers was holding a sales meeting. The sales representatives received a base salary along with their commissions. During a discussion of the recent boom in sales as auto manufacturers outsourced more components, the sales director said with a straight face: "Right now, team, we are facing an internal problem. The president said at our present rate of sales, two of you will soon be earning more than he does. And he doesn't like it. I told the president he could join our team if he could prove to us that he can do the job."

The sales director's comment complimented the outstanding performance of two members of the group. In addition, he added to team pride by pointing out that the sales group is so elite that it was uncertain if the president had the right capabilities to join them.

Effective humor can sometimes insult members of one's own group, but it must avoid insulting outsiders to their face.

Someone who pokes fun at, or even insults, members of his or her own group will be tolerated and laughed along with, but an outsider to the group will not be perceived as funny if he or she makes the same comments. Call it the insider's license. This guideline for workplace humor follows a rule from life outside the office. A black person, for example, might be perceived as funny if he or she made a derogatory joke about blacks when among black people. However, if an Asian made the same joke in the presence of black people, that person would be taken seriously and not accepted at all.

Let's take a workplace example of this principle in action: Larry, an engineer, had returned to work from his honeymoon. At a morning staff meeting, several people asked him how things had gone at the wedding and on his honeymoon vacation. Larry said that the honeymoon went smoothly but that he had run into one glitch at the wedding.

> "One of my bride's uncles came rushing into the church to say that he wanted the ceremony halted because I was an imposter. He said I couldn't really be an engineer. The minister wanted to know the basis for his statement. The uncle said, "Can't you see this man has no plastic pocket protector in his tux. He's not a real engineer."

Being engineers, the rest of the group enjoyed this form of joshing. Yet if a person from marketing or finance had made fun of the fact that engineers sport an omnipresent plastic pocket protector, the reception might have been much less warm.

Effective humor in the workplace should support a serious purpose.

Humor and creativity consultant Lindsay Collier advises his clients to use humor that focuses on and, if possible, supports a serious purpose. By being connected with the task at hand, the humor will be perceived as especially clever, thus contributing to the magnetism of the person making the comment.

A principal in an investment firm told the staff at an 8:30 A.M. meeting: "I wish I had good news to tell you. But the truth is that the economic reports to be released this week show that almost all economic indicators are up. Housing starts are way up, inventories have declined, car sales are up, and consumer confidence has jumped three percentage points. The consequences for our clients should be disastrous."

Perhaps you are wondering why the staff chuckled at the principal's announcement. The explanation is that in recent years, good economic news has typically meant that the major stock markets plunge. Portfolio managers fear that interest rates will climb and stocks will then not have so much of an edge over interest-bearing securities. The comment about the good news bringing bad news for the clients helped prime the investment counselors to meet the challenges of the day. Many clients would be worried about their investments.

Effective humor goes beyond posting cartoons outside your office or cubicle.

Many workers assume that by posting clever cartoons outside their work area, they will develop a reputation for being witty. In recent years, for example, affixing Dilbert cartoons to the wall has become endemic. In fairness to the people who post Dilbert and other cartoons, they often choose those episodes that relate particularly well to a problem in their office. Nevertheless, being perceived as magnetic requires more than posting the cartoons prepared by professionals. You need to supply creative input of your own.

Self-effacing humor is generally the safest bet.

A standard rule for comedians both in the office and onstage is that it is safer to insult yourself than others. Charismatic leaders are masters at mild self-effacement. Ronald Reagan in the later years of his presidency referred to a conversation he had had with Thomas Jefferson during his (Reagan's) youth. A marketing vice president at a consumer electronics company gave the technical writing group this charge: "I want you to make the owner's manual so easy to follow that even I could learn how to operate our microwave ovens."

Self-effacing humor should be light and indulged infrequently to avoid detracting from the humorist's magnetism. Carried to an extreme, self-effacing humor is a form of negative self-talk and will sooner or later begin to pall.

Effective humor minimizes teasing.

My concern about teasing is that it usually is a thinly veiled form of hostility. Teasing others about their physical characteristics, mental ability, or skills is more likely to engender resentment than enhance your magnetism. Teasing others in an attempt at humor can also create enemies. One executive frequently teased a department head about his baldness. One day the board of directors contacted a sample of middle managers about this executive's suitability for promotion to CEO. The middle manager who was teased frequently told the board that "Many people found him to be insulting and insensitive." The executive did not receive the promotion.

Practical jokes and pranks are best avoided.

Practical jokes and pranks have gained in popularity in recent years. Many people receive phony notices that they have been downsized or that a computer virus has destroyed the data they have been collecting for two months. Another finds her attaché case and plant hanging from her office ceiling. Such forms of humor may have positive consequences for the individual and the organization. Yet they do very little to enhance the magnetism of their perpetrators.

One reason practical jokes and pranks do not contribute to magnetism is that they are often anonymous, thus giving you no credit. Another problem is that practical jokes and pranks on the job are looked upon by many people as a sign of immaturity. A high-tech work environment is an exception. A practical joke or prank will be admired if it reflects ingenuity—like floating a vice president's car in a lily pond.

Effective workplace humor makes a point.

Akin to workplace humor supporting a serious purpose, workplace humor should ideally also make a point. The humorous comment should alert another person to the need for change, compliment the person, or help solve an organizational problem. A president asked a middle manager how well her assignment of changing the accounts receivable system was proceeding. She replied, "Pretty well. I've already obtained my first twelve approvals." Ouch! Yet the humorous comment helped the president to recognize how badly the company needed to reengineer its process for making changes in an important system.

How Humor Helps the Organization

Hard evidence and opinion continue to accumulate that humor helps the organization to run more smoothly in various ways. If you use humor to achieve many of these positive consequences, it will add to your reputation as a magnetic and charismatic person. Both co-workers and higher-ranking individuals will be impressed with your results. One explanation offered for the perception of charisma is that it is a direct consequence of a leader's having achieved good results; others then automatically conclude—in a sort of unconscious haloization process—that this person is charismatic. The traditional view is that it is the charisma that leads to outstanding results, not the outstanding results that lead to a perception of charisma.

Here we will run through some of the positive consequences of humor on the job. The more effective your humor, the more likely it is that some of these consequences will be forthcoming.

- *Humor brings people together and helps them cope better with their demanding jobs.* A survey conducted in a Canadian financial services firm asked employees to rate their managers on leadership style and use of humor. Measures of performance were taken a year later. The workers who performed the best more often had managers who made frequent use of humor and who also had other charismatic traits.[3]

- *Effective use of humor on the job typically increases productivity.* One reason for the link between productivity and humor is that humor helps people relax, and they produce more when they are relaxed.

- *Humor in the form of playing around with ideas in a mirthful way encourages creativity.* Humor is a source of intellectual stimulation because the mind has to be stretched to find the amusing element embedded in a work situation. To get the team in a creative mode, the humor-inducing team leader might say, "Pretend you are our product (such as a bicycle). What would you do to improve yourself?"

- *Humor reduces tension.* A hearty laugh is physically relaxing because it tightens muscles, then loosens them. A small nervous laugh, however, may actually increase tension. A hearty laugh is also much like physical exercise. It reduces stress and the accompanying tension because laughter releases endorphins—those hormones that induce a state of relaxation and heightened awareness.

If you have the effect on people of releasing endorphins, your magnetism ratings will surge.

• *Humor, by allowing us to see the lighter side of an issue, helps us keep things in proper perspective.* A claims examiner at Nationwide Insurance apologized profusely to her manager because she had crashed her computer file on a complicated automobile claim. The manager replied, "How horrible. What you have done rivals a flood in terms of how badly Nationwide will be ravaged. We'll both lose our jobs. Now just call the policyholder, explain that you made a mistake, and get the job done." (The claims examiner chuckled and prepared to redo her assignment.)

• *Humor is a potent tool for defusing conflict.* When two individuals or two groups are in conflict with each other, a skilled leader can make a humorous comment that will help both sides resolve their differences. At a telecommunications company, two groups continued to argue about which should have responsibility for which product. At one staff meeting the manager showed up with a bag full of coloring books and crayons. He poured them out onto the table, saying, "So long as we're acting like children about who gets to do what, let's have the right work materials." The light mood helped the two groups to take a less territorial approach to resolving their conflict.

• *Humor is useful in facilitating social relationships.* According to W. Jack Duncan and J. Philip Feisal, *lubricant humor* facilitates relationships and reduces tensions. This type of humor keeps the machinery of interaction running smoothly, and is the type of humor preferred by magnetic individuals. In contrast, *abrasive humor* acts as an irritant to the machinery of interaction. Lubricant humor is an excellent vehicle for helping a person to feel at home in the group.[4]

• *Humor increases job satisfaction and involvement.* David J. Abramis studied 923 workers across a variety of occupations and employers. Of these people, 678 received an extensive questionnaire, and 347 were interviewed at length on many subjects, including fun and humor in the workplace. People who expressed more positive humor at work, such as telling jokes and attempting to make others laugh, rated higher on mental health, job satisfaction, and job involvement. The same people were also less likely to quit.[5]

A personally magnetic manager could help workers achieve the positive outcomes mentioned in this study by being a model of effective humor.

- *The right type of humor helps people cope with adversity.* A while back, Owens-Corning Fiberglass was forced to shut down half its facilities and lay off 40 percent of its workforce to fend off a takeover threat. Anticipating the trauma the layoffs might create, the company hired humor consultant C. W. Metcalf. Over a five-month period, Metcalf presented workshops to about 1,600 employees. He also instructed company trainers on how to maintain a humor program with the help of his videotapes on humor. The adverse effects the company had most feared—violence, sabotage, threats to management, and suicide—did not occur. The humor programs received considerable credit for helping employees manage the trauma of the layoffs.[6]

The link between the Owens-Corning experience and you is that if your group is facing an adverse change, it would be wise to find ways to lighten up the atmosphere. Laugh about little incongruities that happen every day, but shy away from joking about people losing their jobs.

In addition to helping the organization, a good sense of humor can help you advance your career in several ways. As the major theme of this chapter states, an effective sense of humor contributes directly to your magnetism, thus enlarging your potential. Demonstrating a sense of humor can help you get hired. Hodge-Cronin and Associates, an executive search firm, interviewed 737 chief executives about their selection criteria. Of the chief executives surveyed, 98 percent said they would hire a person with a good sense of humor over a straitlaced worker.[7] Similarly, a person is more likely to be promoted into a managerial position if he or she has a sense of humor. The reason is that displaying a sense of humor is a key interpersonal skill.

A Sampler of Magnetic Jokes

Given that jokes contribute much less to magnetism than do witty comments, they should be used sparingly. Nevertheless, there are occasions when a properly timed joke can both enhance your image and help other people and the organization. A key principle is that the joke should have some logical relationship to a problem or challenge faced by the group. If the group is having an image problem with the rest of the organization, find a joke related to a group's image (such as the one presented later). Telling a gross joke or one about the president of the United States would not contribute to the situation or to your image.

A major challenge in telling jokes to introduce humor is that unless you made up the joke, it may be familiar to your listeners. If your listener's extraverbal communication tells you that he or she has heard the joke, stop. In a group setting, you might ask the person who appears to have heard the joke to finish it. Such a maneuver will make you appear magnanimous if not magnetic.

The following five jokes are each headed by the settings in which they might be most relevant:

1. *A work group's image problem caused by outsiders not fully appreciating its contribution.* You may need to reproduce and circulate this one or read it to the group. The following letter makes its way onto many walls in advertising agencies:

> Dear Ann Landers:
>
> I have a problem. I have two brothers. One brother is in advertising. The other was put to death in the electric chair for murder. My mother committed suicide when I was three years old. My two sisters are prostitutes, and my father sells narcotics to high school students. Recently I met a young woman who was just released from jail, where she served time for smothering her newborn child to death. I want to marry her.
>
> My problem is if I marry this woman, should I tell her about my brother who is in advertising?
>
> —S.S.

You can substitute any profession for advertising, and you have a joke that should make the group laugh. If the group is having a problem being accepted by others in the organization, the Ann Landers joke would be a good tension reliever. Assume, for example, that you are a member of a strategic planning group, and many other departments do not understand your role. Substitute "strategic planning" for "advertising" and you will have a winner.

Now assume that you are a member of a group whose contribution is questioned by some people in the organization, and that you are visiting another part of the organization. A vice president of human resources who makes periodic trips to company divisions gets a positive reception with this joke:

> Sorry to be a few minutes late, but I ran into a little difficulty on the way in. One of your security guards stopped me and wouldn't let me through. She claimed I was suspicious looking and wanted to know the nature of my business. When I said "human resources," she responded, "Sounds even more suspicious."

2. *A need for getting relevant information sooner.* If your group could do a better job of obtaining relevant information sooner so it won't be stuck when attempting to complete important tasks. To illustrate the point, try this joke:

> A skydiver jumped from a plane and pulled his rip cord. The parachute did not open. He pulled his emergency parachute rip cord. To his chagrin, there was no parachute.
>
> As he plummeted down, he looked around desperately for some miracle. All of a sudden he spotted a man shooting skyward from the ground.
>
> As they passed each other, the skydiver called out to the skyrocketing man: "What do you know about parachutes?" The man yelled back: "What do you know about gas stoves?"[8]

The joke about two people going in different directions works quite well. People tend to laugh about others facing terrible plights when the scenario is so preposterous that it is not ghoulish. After telling this joke, the leader can say, "Now let's get to the point of how this story relates to us."

3. *The importance of not deceiving customers.* Assume you have noticed several instances in which your co-workers or subordinates have attempted to deceive customers or tell them white lies. As a lead-in to this sensitive topic, consider this story:

> At a big-city airport in the northern United States in January, an airline baggage handler discovered an animal carrier that was left behind. In it was a dog, frozen stiff. His supervisor had the luggage handler locate an almost identical dog from a dog pound and deliver it to the owner.
>
> The woman who owned the dog was stunned and told the baggage handler that the dog was not hers. The airline employee insisted it was. The woman said: "It can't be. My dog died in Florida and I had him frozen to travel here so I could bury him nearby."

Although this joke deals with the death of a pet, it avoids being insensitive to pet owners. The airline baggage handler did nothing to contribute to the death of the dog. Yet both the supervisor and the baggage handler attempted to deceive the passenger. This fact serves as a humorous backdrop for dealing with the problem of treating customers ethically.

4. *The problem of trivializing customer (or patient) complaints.* Up until the late 1950s, the most commonly told jokes were about honeymooners, traveling salesmen, and farmers' daughters. For the past forty-five years jokes about physicians and attorneys have replaced them. Jokes about physicians or other health-care providers can be effective in illustrating the importance of taking customer complaints seriously. Maybe the following story will work for you, and add to your magnetism:

> A man suffering from a painful episode of tennis elbow went to an acupuncturist for treatment. The acupuncturist attempted to cure the problem by placing three needles in the elbow for an hour. That evening the patient had a throbbing pain and called the acupuncturist, complaining that the pain was insufferable. The acupuncturist said: "Take two thumbtacks and call me in the morning."

Why many people laugh so hard at this story (as I hope you did) is that it parodies what is considered the standard medical advice given over the phone, "Take two aspirins and call me in the morning." The story also serves to alert us to the importance of taking customer complaints seriously and offering assistance when needed.

5. *The importance of effective pricing.* A challenge in any business is to offer customers a good price yet still charge enough to maintain reasonable profit margins. If your group is concerned about prices, or costs, or dealing with delicate customer problems, the following story might come in handy:

> A pretzel stand was located in front of an office building in the Wall Street area of New York City. One day, a well-dressed man came out of the building, plunked down fifty cents, and then went on his way without taking a pretzel. The man repeated this unusual act every business day for three weeks.
>
> Finally, the old lady who operated the pretzel stand spoke up: "Sir, excuse me. May I have a word with you?"
>
> The fellow said, "I know what you're going to say. You're going to ask me why I give you fifty cents every day and don't take a pretzel."
>
> The woman replied, "Not at all. I just want to tell you that the price is now seventy-five cents."

The pretzel stand operator story makes people laugh when they think about pricing. Like most good jokes, the story also illustrates that sometimes chutzpah can get out of hand. Don't push your demands too far with a great customer.

A Sampler of Magnetic Witty Comments

A major conclusion about the contribution of humor to magnetism and charisma is that a witty comment is the most effective. A witty comment linked to a specific situation demonstrates to others that you are creative and can think rapidly. Another impressive feature of a witty comment is that it reflects originality. In contrast, with a joke, others may think that you have borrowed it from someone else even when you have developed it yourself.

A witty comment is less fraught with risk than a joke. If you make a witty comment that others do not find funny, the comment will often be accepted as merely a factual statement. You will not be perceived as having told a bad joke. A joke that bombs, however, interferes with the rapport between you and your listeners.

To illustrate the point about a witty comment, suppose you make a trip to your company's facilities in Anchorage, Alaska, the week after Labor Day. You think you are being witty by saying, "I'm glad I arrived here before the frost sets in." In your mind, the humor is that you have grossly exaggerated the weather conditions in Anchorage. Yet the local citizens just interpret your comment as a factual statement. The temperature in Anchorage routinely drops below 32 degrees Fahrenheit (0 degrees Celsius) at night by early September. The situation is not funny; it's just a fact. The comment has as much impact as a visitor to Phoenix, Arizona, in July noting that the temperature is 115 degrees Fahrenheit (43 degrees Celsius).

Here is a sampling of five witty comments that helped the person making the comment to establish better rapport with the group. As with the illustrative jokes, these are largely situation-specific:

1. *Dealing with having been promoted over co-workers.* Consultant Barbara Mackoff recalls how a manager who had recently been promoted to supervise her former co-workers relabeled a tense situation. The manager began her first meeting with the comment, "Now I don't want you to think of me as your boss. I want you to think of me as your friend." Then she paused and smiled and proceeded. "Think of me as your friend who is always right." The manager's playful icebreaker contributed substantially to gaining the cooperation of the group.[9]

2. *Explaining to others why you received a big promotion.* Closely related to the above is the problem of justifying to others why you received a promotion when co-workers also had good qualifications. I. C. (Ishwer Chhabildas) Shah is a prominent businessperson in the telecommunications field whose native country is India. Years back, while an employee of Xerox Corp., he was promoted to a key product manager position.

According to Shah, he told potentially jealous co-workers that the Xerox marketing vice president had chosen him because the product had too many chiefs and not enough Indians. As a kicker, Shah added, "I told them my name I. C. meant 'Indian Chief.' "

3. *Bringing relief to a somber atmosphere.* At one somber meeting, the company president talked about the possible liquidation

of the organization. The silence that followed seemed to last an eternity. At that point, the director of systems development turned to the head of engineering, who had just returned from vacation and was visibly sunburned. "Tell us, Peg," he said, "did you use suntan lotion or barbecue sauce while you were at the beach?" Laughter erupted, tension plummeted, and the president was able to proceed with a frank discussion of how they would deal with the company's problems."[10]

Somber atmospheres are so frequent in business that a second witty comment appropriate to this category would not be amiss. During a troubled period at ITT, a senior financial executive began by sketching an ocean liner on a flip chart. Next, he printed on a larger scale the letters *ITT.* The other members of the team stared intently and burst into laughter when the executive added six more letters to form the word *ITTitanic.* The link between the fate of the *Titanic* and the exaggerated possible fate of ITT brought laugher and a realization that the meeting would be addressing a serious problem.

4. *Pointing out the need for change.* Witty comments can be effective in getting others to understand the need for change when a confrontation might be harsher than the situation warrants. Humor used in this way can be an effective influence tactic for the magnetic manager. Here is how one top manager used a witty comment to make a criticism:

> A fastidious executive toured the company's office facilities. During her trip, she noticed several instances of coffee pots and small microwave ovens in the work area—a violation of safety regulations. The executive commented to the office manager, "In general, I like what I see, but why have our employees set up light housekeeping? Are you keeping them here all hours of the night?" Not long after, the gear for food and beverage preparation was no longer present except in the employee lounge.

The witty comment about light housekeeping was thus an effective influence tactic. Of course, the executive delivered the comment with a warm facial expression and smile. The right extraverbal signals are an essential part of wit.

5. *Poking fun at oneself.* A bald manager was conducting a meeting on developing a mission statement for the group. Ten minutes into the meeting, a maintenance worker entered the room to change a fluorescent bulb that was flickering. Attention was drawn to the worker as he climbed the ladder and began removing the bulb. Sensing that he was disrupting the meeting, the worker said, "Don't worry. I'll be out of your hair in a moment." The manager retorted, "It's nice to know that you will be finished soon. But you weren't in my hair. It's a physical impossibility." At this, the team members burst into spontaneous laughter, which helped bring them together more closely. By gently poking fun at himself, the team leader was following an important tenet of effective humor.

Suggestions for Becoming Funnier

The ideas presented so far are geared toward improving your use of humor. Regard the following suggestions as a program for further developing your sense of humor so as to enhance your magnetism and charisma.[11]

- *Pinpoint the situations that make you laugh.* Attempt to understand the factors in those situations that you found funny.
- *Try to believe that the world is out to do you good rather than its being against you.* With a positive expectation, it is easier to see the humor in everyday events.
- *Become more playful.* Developmental psychologist Paul McGhee says: "Learn to recognize and combat terminal seriousness by taking a playful approach to what you are doing."
- *Maintain a humor notebook or computer file.* Fill it with funny sayings, good jokes, humorous situations, and amusing statements and actions by children. Categorize your file by topic. Surf the Internet for humorous material.
- *Regularly invest time in studying humor.* Watch comedians on television, read books and articles about humor, and attempt to observe what makes people laugh in everyday situations.
- *Smile and laugh more frequently, but not to the point of frivolousness.* If you practice smiling and laughing frequently it will become integrated into your repertoire.

• *Whenever you use humor on the job, keep it relevant to the purpose at hand.* Otherwise humor becomes a distraction and does not add to your stature.

• *To obtain material for self-effacing humor, reflect on your weaknesses, eccentricities, and fanatical attitudes.* If you are willing to share these with others, you have an opportunity for showing your capacity to laugh at yourself.

• *Follow the lead of professional comedians by practicing jokes with friends and family before using them on your intended audience.* If your family members laugh, you will know for sure that your delivery and extraverbal behavior pass muster.

• *Develop the right mental set for making witty comments by practicing them in a variety of settings.* Develop witty comments about shopping in the supermarket, walking through the shopping malls, driving through traffic, waiting to use an ATM, or having your hair done.

• *Create puns from time to time if only because they heighten your ability to play with language and find mirthful patterns.*

• *Observe the witty comments and delivery of comedians and others appearing on television.* You may not want to emulate these people, but you will probably pick up a few good ideas.

To get started strengthening your skills in humor, do the accompanying exercise. Activities of this nature are an important supplement to the suggestions just made.

Practicing Your Sense of Humor

Make a witty comment relevant to the following scenarios. Force yourself to come up with something, even if it isn't as funny as you would like.

1. Five minutes before entering your weekly staff meeting, you are informed by top management that all salary adjustments will be suspended for one year. You had planned to devote your staff meeting to emphasizing the need for increased productivity.
2. One of your co-workers informs you that her son flunked out

of his second year of college because he spent so much time surfing the Internet that he hardly ever studied or attended class.

3. The vice president of marketing has just been replaced by her assistant, who is half her age and someone she had mentored for several years.

Illustrative witty comments for these three scenarios can be found at the end of the book before the references.

In this chapter we have taken an analytical look at humor with the purpose of helping you to use humor to enhance your magnetism and charisma. I began by analyzing why humor is funny and what the characteristics of effective humor are. I then explained how humor benefits the organization, thus adding to the stature of the person who provided the humor, and went on to present samples of magnetic jokes and witty comments, followed by some direct suggestions for becoming funnier.

You are now positioned to learn about a technical approach to becoming more magnetic and charismatic.

9

Achieving Magnetism Through Neurolinguistic Programming

Personal magnetism can also be viewed as a by-product of excelling in many important domains in life. If you excel in such areas as communicating, motivating, influencing, negotiating, and leading others, you are personally magnetic. A field of study developed in recent years, called neurolinguistic programming (NLP), attempts to identify what works in thinking, language use, and behavior. It is a way of identifying and reproducing excellence that enables people to consistently achieve the results they want in their careers and personal lives. NLP is also the study of exceptional talent.

Perhaps the promises of NLP are exaggerated, or perhaps not. My purpose here is to describe several aspects of neurolinguistic programming that could help you to become a more influential and magnetic person.[1] Regard these aspects of NLP as additional techniques available toward achieving a magnetic and charismatic impact. Before digging into those aspects of NLP that are particularly useful for enhancing magnetism, however, I should first explain more precisely what this field is all about.

The Components of Neurolinguistic Programming

NLP is a fast-growing branch of applied psychology and communication. It attempts to pinpoint why some people are more gifted than others in terms of what they do differently. By studying NLP you can learn these patterns of excellence. According to neurolinguistic programming, three basic ideas are essential for understanding how humans think and behave:

1. *Neuro* refers to the neurological or nervous system. It is the way people use the sense of sight, hearing, touch, taste, and smell to translate experience into thoughts, both conscious and unconscious. Magnetic people appear to have a high level of sensory awareness, and therefore are more observant with all their senses. The *neuro* is also about how a person's mind and physiology work together to form a system. NLP aims to help you to increase your awareness of your neurological system and to use it more to your advantage.
2. *Linguistic* is about how people use language to make sense of their experience and how people communicate that experience to themselves and others. Language patterns are an expression of who a person is and how he or she thinks. Magnetic individuals are linguistically superior to others. As described earlier, they display a masterful, colorful communication style.
3. *Programming* refers to the coding of experience. A program is a series of step developed to achieve a specific goal or result. You can also regard a program as a systematic technique or a way of organizing ideas and actions to achieve results. If you become aware of the programs that work best for yourself, you can repeat them for continued success.

In short, NLP deals with three aspects of human functioning: (1) how we organize what we receive with our senses; (2) how we use language to describe our sensory input; and (3) how we act both intentionally and unintentionally to produce results.

With this brief introduction into the meaning of NLP, you are now prepared to apply it in several ways to enhance your magnetism and charisma.

Enriching Your Communication Through Sensory-Rich Language

A major contribution of NLP to magnetism is the emphasis it places on the language of successful people. Early research in the field revealed that skilled communicators use language in a way that creates a climate of trust and understanding. Effective communicators intuitively adapt their language to the language of their influence targets. The effective communicator will search for words and phrases that evoke emotion in others. For example, in attempting to influence single parents, the communicator would make frequent reference to such ideas as work-family conflict, leading a balanced life, and nontraditional families.

Using the right buzzwords to establish rapport has been a well-established principle of persuasive communication long before neurolinguistic programming came along. A more unique contribution of NLP is to point you toward using sensory-specific language. Verbal communication typically concentrates on three modes: the visual, the auditory, and the kinesthetic, better known as the feelings. If you size up the preferred mode of your influence target, you can slant more of your communication toward his or her preferred mode.

People who think visually will often use such expressions as the following to reflect their preferred mode of communication:

- "I see what you're talking about."
- "I get the picture."
- "I see what you mean."
- "I have a much better focus on what you are saying."
- "What you say is clear to me now."

People who think in an auditory mode will frequently use these expressions:

- "Sounds good to me."
- "I hear what you are saying."
- "Do you hear me?"
- "That sound's important."
- "If I'm hearing you correctly."

People who think in a feeling mode are more likely to use expressions of this type:

- "I feel we are communicating."
- "What you say moves me."

- "This situation grates on my nerves."
- "I don't want to come down hard on you."
- "You have a solid grasp of the situation."

Although the visual, auditory, and feeling modes are dominant, the sensory modes of taste and smell can also be incorporated into speech to communicate more effectively:

- "My dealings with him left a bad taste in my mouth."
- "I can taste victory."
- "I smell something rotten here."
- "Your suggestion has the aroma of success."
- "The whole deal has a good scent."

The personally magnetic individual appeals to multiple senses, as described in Chapter 2. He or she will therefore make extensive use of sensory language. To continue further with your development of sensory language, study the following list of representative words under each of the three sensory modes:

Visual	**Auditory**	**Feelings**
look	say	touch
picture	hear	handle
imagine	talk	impact
visualize	discuss	relax
perspective	quiet	tough
reveal	shrill	scrape
see	deaf	solid
view	snap	heavy
fuzzy	bang	smooth
watch	clip	rough

Awareness of sensory words leads naturally to an awareness of sensory phrases. The use of phrases loaded with sensory language enhances magnetism. If your choice of sensory words and phrases matches the preferred mode of your influence target, your magnetic impact will be even stronger. Here is a sampling of expressions for each of the three major sensory modes:

Visual

I can see clearly now.
I am looking closely at your idea.
I take a dim view of that course of action.
She is a sight for sore eyes.
He has a blind spot.
It appears to me.
In my mind's eye.
I hope this will illuminate the problem.
I can just see it.
Beyond a shadow of a doubt.

Auditory

I can hear it now.
Don't turn a deaf ear to my problem.
What you say is music to my ears.
Just listen to yourself.
What you say is loud and clear.
That rings a bell.
We're in tune with each other.
Tell me exactly what you mean.
We must silence that report.
I can hear the applause now.

Feelings

Sharp as a tack.
That really hurts.
We may have to knock heads.
I grasp what you say.
Give her my warmest regards.
I can't put my finger on it.
He's a smooth operator.
We must get a handle on the problem.
He is thick-skinned.
We haven't yet scratched the surface.

To further raise your awareness level of the use of sensory language by charismatic people, I next offer an excerpt from an interview with master negotiator Herb Cohen. Most people who have seen Cohen in action would describe him as magnetic and charismatic. He charms and convinces his influence targets with a combination of wit, common sense, and penetrating insights. As you read the excerpt, look for examples of sensory language, initialing them *V* (visual), *A* (auditory), or *F* (feelings):

Question: What do top salespeople and top negotiators have in common?

Cohen: Real pros in both fields transform initial noes into yeses. A salesperson should never accept an initial no—it's only the other side's opening bid. People tend to say no whenever they're presented with a new idea that they haven't had time to think through. You're asking them to take a risk, and it's human nature to be risk-averse.

To change the no to yes, come back to them when they've had time to think about your offer and time to ask around about you. Help them spread the risk by suggesting they buy a small amount of what you're offering to get started, or change the initial terms modestly in another way.

Question: Is the customer always right?

Cohen: No, but let him think he is. If a customer says something really stupid, respond by saying something that sounds a little self-deprecating: "Based on my narrow perspective, this is how I see it." The last thing you want to think to yourself is, "I guess I'll have to educate this moron."[2]

Next we repeat the excerpt, with the addition of visual (*V*), auditory (*A*), and feelings (*F*) notations. in comparing your analysis with mine, do not expect complete agreement. There is an element of subjectivity in analyzing sensory modes as revealed by speech.

Question: What do top salespeople and top negotiators have in common?

Cohen: Real pros in both fields transform (*F*) initial noes into yeses. A salesperson should never accept (*V*) an initial no—it's only the other side's opening bid. People tend to say (*A*) no whenever they're presented (*V*) with a new idea (*V*) that they haven't had time to think (*V*) through. You're asking (*A*) them to take a risk, and it's human nature to be risk-averse (*V*).

To change (*F*) the no to yes, come back to them when they've had time to think (*V*) about your offer and time to ask (*A*) around about you. Help them spread (*F*) the risk by suggesting (*A*) they buy a small amount of what you're offering to get started, or change (*F*) the initial terms modestly in another way.

Question: Is the customer always right?

Cohen: No, but let him think (*V*) he is. If a customer says (*A*) something really stupid, respond (*A*) by saying (*A*) something that sounds (*A*) a little self-deprecating: "Based on my narrow perspective, this is how I see (*V*) it." The last thing you want to think (*V*) to yourself is, "I guess I'll have to educate this moron."

To acquire insight into your sensory mode preferences, take the accompanying quiz. The quiz will also help you to raise your awareness level and facilitate incorporating sensory-rich ideas into your thinking and speaking.

Identifying Your Preferred Thinking Pattern

For each of the following categories, think about the item, person, or place listed and check the element or elements that come to mind.[3]

1. Gasoline
   a. An image of some sort (such as a car or service station)
   b. A sound (such as the sound of gas pouring into a tank or a bell ringing inside the station)
   c. A touch (such as the cool feel of the gas pump handle)
   d. A smell (such as the odor of the gas)
   e. A taste (such as the taste in your mouth after exposure to the gasoline fumes)
2. Your best friend
   a. A sound (such as the sound of the friend's voice)

   b. An emotion (such as your feelings toward him or her)
   c. A smell (such as the friend's perfume or cologne)
   d. A taste (such as a meal you ate with this friend)
   e. An image (such as what the friend looks like or a place you have visited with that person)
3. The way you would like to spend your time
   a. The sounds associated with the activity (such as the sound of people's voices)
   b. A taste (such as the taste of a particular food)
   c. A smell (such as the aroma of your environment)
   d. An image (such as the place you would like to be)
   e. An emotion (such as how you feel when you think of spending your time this way)
4. What you did yesterday
   a. A taste of some sort (such as what you ate)
   b. An image or a picture (such as the scene of where you were)
   c. A sound or conversation
   d. A touch, sensation, or emotion (such as your touching somebody or something)
   e. A smell (such as the smell of a restaurant)
5. A time you didn't enjoy very much
   a. A smell (such as the exhaust fumes from a bus)
   b. A sound (such as what you heard or what you were saying to yourself)
   c. A taste (such as swallowing salt water while swimming)
   d. An image (such as what was happening or what you could imagine)
   e. A touch or emotion (a negative emotion you had at the time)
6. Your favorite restaurant
   a. A touch or emotion (how you feel being there)
   b. What you see (such as the people you are with, the decor of the restaurant)
   c. What you hear (such as the conversation, the music)
   d. A taste (such as the taste of the steak you ordered or of a beverage)
   e. A smell (such as the aroma from the kitchen)
7. Something from your early childhood
   a. A smell (such as your mother's perfume or the mustiness of an attic)

   b. A touch or an emotion (such as when your father carried you piggyback)
   c. An image (such as picturing yourself in a playground)
   d. Sounds or voices (such as children yelling in a swimming pool)
   e. A taste (such as that of a home-cooked meal)
8. Your work
   a. A sound (such as that from equipment or voices)
   b. An image (such as a mental picture of what you do)
   c. A taste (such as the taste in your mouth when you lick stamps)
   d. A smell (such as new carpeting exudes)
   e. A touch or an emotion (such as what you feel about your work)
9. Where you might be tomorrow
   a. An image or a picture (such as of a park or a building)
   b. An emotion or touch (such as feeling lonely or shaking hands with an interesting person)
   c. A taste (such as the taste of a hot dog or an Italian sausage)
   d. A smell or aroma (such as that from flowers sold outside a building)
   e. A sound (such as the blast from a construction site)
10. Something you find difficult to do
   a. An image or picture (such as of parallel parking)
   b. A taste (such as from eating rabbit or eels)
   c. A sound or conversation (such as singing)
   d. An associated emotion or touch (such as attending a funeral)
   e. A smell (such as the one associated with visiting a hospital)
11. Something you find rewarding
   a. An emotion (such as a feeling of satisfaction or the sensation of striking a ball correctly)
   b. A taste (such as that of your favorite food)
   c. A smell (such as that of a nice person's perfume or cologne)
   d. A sound (such as what you say to yourself or the sound of children's voices in your environment).
   e. An image (such as what the rewarding experience looks like)
12. Something you find amusing
   a. A sound (such as what someone says or what you hear)
   b. An image (something or someone you see)
   c. An emotion (such as the relaxed feeling throughout your body)

d. A taste (such as the fizzle in a carbonated beverage)
e. A smell (such as the aroma of baby powder)

Analysis of Thinking Patterns: Circle the letters you chose for each answer.

	Visual	*Auditory*	*Feelings*	*Taste*	*Smell*
1.	a	b	c	e	d
2.	e	a	b	d	c
3.	d	a	e	b	c
4.	b	c	d	a	e
5.	d	b	e	c	a
6.	b	c	a	d	e
7.	c	d	b	e	a
8.	b	a	e	c	d
9.	a	e	b	c	d
10.	a	c	d	b	e
11.	e	d	a	b	c
12.	b	a	c	d	e
Totals	—	—	—	—	—

Now add the number of letters circled in each column. These scores indicate your preference in thinking pattern (or sensory mode). The higher the score, the more likely you are to use this sense as a way of processing information. There are no right answers.

Establishing Rapport Through a Climate of Trust

Personally magnetic people are remarkably good at establishing rapport with others they meet for the first time. Furthermore, they are able to maintain this rapport in future contacts. Given that the ability to establish rapport is so closely linked to magnetism, any gains you can make in building rapport with others will enhance your impact on them. Neurolinguistic programming has much to offer in this regard. Its best-known and most widely practiced techniques focus on building rapport or empathy with others.

From the perspective of NLP, rapport is the ability to relate to others in a manner that creates a climate of trust and understanding. So if you build rapport with others, you are not being manipulative or unethical: You are creating genuine understanding.

Matching to Establish Rapport

A starting point in understanding how to build rapport is to observe pairs of people who have good rapport. Begin by thinking of a person with whom you have excellent rapport. What is different about your contact with this person? In what way do you relate to others differently? Have you noticed that you tend to touch each other at the same time? (An example is that two people in good rapport often exchange affectionate punches on the upper arm.) Have you noticed the excellent eye contact you have with this person? Have you noticed how you sigh or laugh at the same time?

If you've been in a very long-term relationship with someone, such as your spouse, others may have told you that you look alike. This perception stems in part from the fact that your physical and facial movements are so much in synch that it creates an illusion of similarity.

The physical matching that takes place between two people who have established rapport is often accompanied by a mental matching. Close business partners note that they often finish each other's sentences. Finishing someone else's sentence may be considered rude in general, but it also indicates rapport. During the fast-growth days at Apple Computer Corp., when Steven Jobs and John Sculley were key players, the pair commented that they usually knew what the other was thinking. Jobs and Sculley ultimately had a bitter split, indicating that intense rapport may not last a lifetime.

A deep level of rapport has occurred when the two people in the interaction adopt the same or similar style in the following aspects of behavior:

- Posture (such as both sitting erect or slouching)
- Facial movements and hand gestures
- Breathing rate and breathing sounds
- Voice tone and quality
- Language content, such as choice of key expressions, expletives, analogies, and clichés

- Choice of sensory modes (visual, auditory, feelings, taste, and smell)
- Beliefs (such as a belief in the scientific method, quantitative evidence, government regulation, or religion)
- Values (such as the importance of family, long-term relationships, money, or recreation)

The more of these dimensions of behavior and thinking you have in common with another individual, the better the matching is. The better the matching and the better the rapport are the greater the magnetic effect upon the other person will be.

How to Match (or Mirror) Another Person

Better rapport with another person can be achieved if you match the individual in several domains. Matching requires that you carefully concentrate on key aspects of the other person's behavior and language, and then reproduce in a natural way what the other person is doing. If the other person, for example, raises her arm and then rests her chin on her thumb and first finger, you do the same. If your influence target sighs, you sigh. And if she smiles, you smile (the easiest thing to match).

But here's the rub: Match in a gentle, natural way. Do not use an exaggerated form of matching such as second graders playing Simon Says would. Match the other person, but avoid aping or appearing to mock him or her. An outright mimic creates the impression of being the sleaziest of office politicians. Two NLP experts explain that "Matching is not mimicry, which is noticeable, exaggerated, and indiscriminate copying of another person's movements, and is usually considered offensive."[4]

Research on building rapport indicates that it is most effective to match as many as possible of the following communication modes:

1. *Posture.* Note the position of the other person's body, the position of the legs and feet and their weight distribution. Does your target put more weight on the left foot or the right foot? What is the position of the arms, hands, and fingers? For example, does

your target rest his hands clenched on the arms of his chair? How are the shoulders held? What is the inclination of the head?

2. *Expression.* What is the direction of the person's look? Where does your target move her gaze? Does she look happy, sad, worried, bored, or ill at ease? Are her lips pursed, or are they open, revealing her teeth?

3. *Breathing.* Pay particular attention to breathing patterns because many NLP specialists believe that matching breathing patterns affords the best opportunity for establishing rapport. Observe carefully the rate of breathing. (If he pants, you pant without being too obvious!) Take mental note of the position of the breathing. Does your influence target breathe from the chest and abdomen or from the lower stomach? (This is much harder to observe than breathing rate.)

4. *Movement.* Everyone has a characteristic rhythm. Carefully match his or her pace. Does the person move rapidly, steadily, or slowly, or does your target remain relatively still? (You may have a difficult time keeping pace with a target who has an attention-deficit disorder.)

5. *Voice.* Observe your influence target's pace, volume, pitch, tone, intonation, and type of words used. Listen to the person's regional accent. If he uses a flat *a,* make your *a*'s a little flatter. If he uses a hard *g* or no *g*'s at all, move lightly in that direction. A heavy imitation of another person's accent will usually be perceived as mockery. The vast majority of people are convinced that they speak the ideal form of their language, while believing that anyone who does not speak as they do has an "accent."

6. *Language patterns as reflected in the sensory mode.* Listen primarily for the visual, auditory, and feeling modes. Listen secondarily for the taste and smell modes. Suppose your influence target says, "I see a big improvement in the near future." Shortly thereafter you might say something to the effect, "I too have a mental picture of good times ahead."

Matching your influence target in the six communication modes just mentioned works effectively in building rapport up to a certain point. A deeper and longer-lasting rapport is achieved when you match with the other person on beliefs and values. Suppose your influence target believes strongly in solving problems through intuition. You will establish better rapport if you can show that you believe likewise. In contrast, if you make frequent mention of the importance of data collection in solving problems, your chances for rapport will diminish.

An effective way to incorporate matching into your magnetism tool kit is to begin small. Start with a form of matching that you think would be natural for you, such as smiling when another person smiles. Try matching smiles for a week. Next, attempt a communication mode slightly more challenging, such as matching the voice volume of another person. Experiment with a neighbor or a store associate. How about trying a match with the representative of your package delivery service? Or your office-equipment repair technician?

Although many people laugh when they first hear about the utility of imitating the breathing pattern of another person, give it a try. Matching another's breathing pattern brings about rapport at a mental and physiological level, thus sharpening your ability to influence others.

As you develop skill in matching others in the domains that appear the most natural to you, practice a more difficult match, such as a person's language pattern. If the person emphasizes the visual mode, you do likewise. Similarly for the auditory, feelings, taste, or smell modes. Your influence target might say, "I can almost taste a bagel right now." You respond, "Yes, don't you just love the crunchy sensation of biting a fresh bagel?"

It is possible to practice the matching technique even when you are not conversing with another person. For example, mirror the behavior of the team leader while sitting at a meeting.

Pacing to Establish Rapport

Another form of matching for rapport is to *pace* another individual. To pace is to respect the emotional state of another individual by showing that you understand his or her state. Pacing has always been a part of a sales representative's tool kit. The skilled salesperson does not argue with an objection but, to the contrary, communicates understanding. After communicating understanding, the salesperson explains how his or her proposition will meet the objection. The customer then might say, "Your product is what we need, but the price is way too high."

To overcome this objection, the salesperson might say, "I understand that you are concerned about price. It is always an important factor. Yet I would like you to consider the long-term cost of using our product. Since it lasts 50 percent longer than competitive products, the true cost of our product is actually lower than what you have been accustomed to paying."

To apply the pacing technique, first be confident that you understand your influence target's emotional state or feelings. If you pick up the slightest hint that the person is angry, listen again for more evidence of anger. If the person has light or medium skin color, watch for the redness that derives from an increased blood flow to the skin when someone is angry. Look for signs of teeth gnashing or a menacing grimace. If you are convinced that the person is angry, you might then make a calming comment such as "I don't blame you for being angry. I would be angry too if I were in your situation."

Pacing also works well with positive states. If you have sufficient evidence that the person is in a mirthful mood, you might respond, "I'm happy you're feeling great. So am I. Let's celebrate."

Pacing is simply another way of establishing rapport by communicating empathy. Every empathic person will not be perceived as magnetic, yet being empathic contributes to your personal magnetism. A company employee said to a vice president in her company: "I'm retiring next month, so what I am going to say is not to gain points with you. I want to tell you that a couple of my friends and I think you are the nicest executive in the company."

The vice president responded, "I'm happy to hear that. But it would be helpful to me to know what I do that people think is so nice." The employee responded, "Remember the day of the big rainstorm two weeks ago? You actually *thanked* us for coming to work despite the storm. Not many other executives would acknowledge what a struggle it was to get to work that day."

Total Body Listening for Rapport

Yet another technique for establishing rapport identified by NLP is *total body listening.* Any type of effective listening helps establish rapport between you and your influence target. Total body listening is listening carried to a higher plane. While listening, you concentrate as much as you can on the other person without being preoccupied with your own thoughts. You become so deeply involved in what the other person is saying that you temporarily put aside your own agenda. Whole body listening is generally similar to the listening recommended for flattering people in Chapter 5.

A unique feature of whole body listening is that you match your posture to that of your influence target. Based on the posture match, the person feels even better understood than with other forms of effective listening. And the better understood a person feels, the more likely it is that he or she will perceive you as personally magnetic.

In this chapter, I have explained how certain aspects of neurolinguistic programming can enhance personal magnetism, such as enriching your language by using sensory-rich words and phrases. The most frequent modes are visual, auditory, and feelings. Yet you can also add smell and taste. You took a quiz to help you identify your preferred communication modes.

The focus here has been on using NLP to establish rapport. The major approach is to match or mirror your influence targets. To do this you gently match these communication modes:

- Posture
- Expression
- Breathing
- Movement
- Voice
- Language patterns

Two other useful ways of establishing rapport are through pacing and total body listening. Both require heavy empathy on your part.

Next we look at a subtle yet powerful way of projecting magnetism and charisma. It would be difficult to sustain your magnetism if you neglected this domain.

10

Displaying Personal Magnetism Through Your Work

Personal magnetism transcends having an attractive physical appearance, a sensational handshake, or a constellation of warm, captivating personality characteristics. Magnetism can also be expressed through one's work. Truly magnetic people are typically passionate about their work. Magnetic people are often envied for the intense joy they find in doing what they are paid to do. The excitement magnetic people derive from their work draws the attention of others.

Before delving into the various ways in which magnetism can be displayed through work, you should first take the accompanying quiz about work attitudes. It will help you to think through some of the issues involved in whether work is a force for personal magnetism in your life.

The Work Attitude Quiz

Indicate how well you agree with the following statements by circling the appropriate response: strongly disagree (**SD**); disagree (**D**); neutral (**N**); agree (**A**); or strongly agree (**SA**).

	SD	D	N	A	SA
1. My work is a direct expression of me.	1	2	3	4	5
2. Sometimes I'm oblivious to the rest of the world when I'm working.	1	2	3	4	5

	SD	D	N	A	SA
3. There are times when I am so absorbed in my work that I forget to stop for food breaks.	1	2	3	4	5
4. I often get drowsy at work.	5	4	3	2	1
5. The best part of my work is the fact that I get paid.	5	4	3	2	1
6. My work is a source of major thrills in my life.	1	2	3	4	5
7. My desk is sloppy.	5	4	3	2	1
8. My use of the computer so far hasn't led to a big improvement in my productivity.	5	4	3	2	1
9. My projects are almost always finished on time.	1	2	3	4	5
10. My work is like a hobby to me.	1	2	3	4	5
11. At times in my life when I was lonely, my work has been a solace to me.	1	2	3	4	5
12. Others marvel at my efficiency.	1	2	3	4	5
13. I don't recall a boss of mine complimenting me on my dedication to work.	5	4	3	2	1
14. Watching my favorite shows (including news and sports) on television is more exciting to me than my work.	5	4	3	2	1
15. At the start of most workdays, I tingle with excitement.	1	2	3	4	5

Score ______

Scoring and Interpretation: Add the numbers you have circled, then look at the interpretation for the range into which you fall.

60–75 You are so passionate about your work that it probably adds to your personal magnetism.

46–59 There are times when your work attitudes and approach to work contribute to others perceiving you as personally magnetic, but the tendency is not pronounced.

15–45 The way in which you perform your work, and your attitudes toward work, very likely detract from the magnetic image you want to project. Another job in which you could become more passionate about your work might enhance your personal magnetism.

Strive for Peak Performance

At their best, personally magnetic individuals experience peak performance, or a total absorption in what they are doing at the time. It is this total absorption that is largely responsible for performing at close to one's capacity. Such people concentrate so fully that the task at hand is virtually their only reality while they are at it. The total absorption and love of the task project magnetism, as does the sight of an expert baton twirler totally absorbed in his or her performance. Let's look at the attributes of peak performers and at how one can achieve the flow experience.

Attributes of Peak Performers

A starting point in understanding how to achieve the flow experience is to examine the attributes of peak performers—those characteristics that are typical of people who regularly experience flow.[1] The flow experience refers to a total absorption in what you are doing at the moment. As you read about these characteristics, observe how they can also contribute to magnetism.

1. *A sense of mission.* Peak performers almost always have a sense of mission. They strive for a broader purpose and motivate others with their mission. The mission of a powerful and wealthy person might seem more exciting, but people in modest positions also have impressive, motivational missions. I know the director of a summer youth program who inspires his workers to provide programs that are so educational and stimulating that the programs have developed a citywide reputation.

2. *Concern about results and processes.* Peak performers obviously want to achieve outstanding results, so they set high goals consistent with their mission. Yet they also care about how they achieve these results. The peak performer cares about the minute

details involved and shows an artist's concern for every part of a project.

3. *Mental and physical calmness.* Perhaps the most remarkable attribute of peak performers is their mental and physical calmness as they proceed with their work. While focusing on the task they love, they are at ease. The ease and calmness of peak performers adds to their magnetic appeal. It is impressive to observe somebody producing outstanding results so calmly.

Think of those moments when you are at your being your absolute best in performing some task. Reflect on your calmness as you tied a rope knot to anchor a boat, effortlessly refinished a table top, or joyfully located a difficult-to-access file from the Internet. You were probably so absorbed in the task that you experienced no distractions, no mental static.

4. *Great powers of concentration.* Mental and physical calmness enable the peak performer to do what is necessary to achieve peak performance, that is, concentrate intently. An ability to concentrate intently contributes mightily to magnetism because others will be impressed by your focus.

5. *Sensory acuity.* Being mentally and physically calm also assists the peak performer in sensing and responding to relevant clues from the environment. Sensory acuity includes all the senses mentioned in Chapter 9 in relation to neurolinguistic programming. Although the peak performer experiences total concentration, he or she will still respond to important signals. For example, the peak-performing sales representative will detect a prospect's facial expression that tells him the time is not quite right to say, "I have the contract ready for you to sign." Instead he might say, "I think we should talk about any other concerns you may have concerning committing yourself."

6. *A results orientation.* To achieve peak performance, a person must produce meaningful results. As obvious as this statement may seem, think about all the people you know who work hard yet produce very little. Around the office these people conduct a lot of meetings, produce exquisite graphics on their computer, and talk impressively—yet useful output is hard to find. Around the house, people who are not results-oriented are often busily engaged in many projects, to the point where they have difficulty

reading because they are so preoccupied with household tasks. Yet their home is no cleaner or neater than most, and they entertain infrequently. The peak performer focuses on meaningful goals, as does the magnetic person.

7. *An ability to correct course.* Peak performers can sense when they are off course. The peak performer senses when she has strayed from the best path toward goal attainment and then redirects her activity. The ability to process feedback from the environment is an important part of knowing when you are off course.

> Monique Gingras is a charming and entertaining woman who operates a successful jewelry store in the face of heavy competition. The backbone of her business is repeat customers who return frequently to receive her individualized attention and advice.
>
> During the start-up phase of her business, Monique was satisfied with, but not ecstatic about, its sales volume. In hopes of increasing sales, Monique decided to display merchandise besides jewelry. She reasoned that since she had excess display space, selling other lines of merchandise would be highly profitable. Monique purchased a line of silk scarves, monogrammed handkerchiefs, and figurines. The new merchandise moved slowly, and jewelry sales also dipped slightly.
>
> Monique attempted to understand why sales were not improving despite the new merchandise line. She decided to listen intently to customer comments about her merchandise. As she listened, Monique picked up some valuable feedback. A few customers murmured something to the effect, "Why is a jewelry store selling this stuff (the scarves, handkerchiefs, and figurines)?" On the basis of this feedback, Monique decided to sell jewelry, watches, and fine pens and pencils, exclusively. In this way she would avoid confusing her store's image. Business volume gradually improved to a level that pleased Monique. Sticking to her core business, and emphasizing her charm, led Monique back on the path to success.

8. *A penchant for self-management.* Peak performers practice self-management; they achieve the results they want without constant prodding from a supervisor. Performance psychologist Charles Garfield summarizes this attribute in these words: "Employees who look for direction every time they have to make a

move are a hindrance to their organizations and themselves. The rising stars are those individuals who can align their own missions with an organization's mission, keep their motivation refreshed by achievement, aim for results, and manage themselves."[2]

How to Achieve the Flow Experience

The flow experience is akin to "being in the zone" in athletics. When you are in the zone you are achieving peak performance largely because your concentration is so complete. When the flow occurs, things go just right. You feel alive and fully attentive to what you are doing. In flow, there is a sense of being lost in the action. The common features of flow experience are high challenge, clear goals, a focus on psychic energy and attention, and continuous feedback.

Flow also involves a loss of self-consciousness. If you are experiencing flow, you are not concerned with yourself at the moment. A person who experiences flow is well-motivated, whether or not status, prestige, or large amounts of money are associated with the job.

Flow contributes to personal magnetism in the most natural way. Instead of being concerned with your image, you project excitement as you go about your work. If you are a sports fan, watch your favorite coach during a big game. He will be so absorbed in the action that people in the crowd cannot distract him. If you are a music fan, observe your favorite conductor or band leader, who will have the same total absorption.

Flow is experienced frequently by people involved in creative work or in sports. A singer is often totally absorbed in his or her singing. A soccer player may receive total enjoyment from stiffening his neck and then passing a ball downfield by allowing the ball to rebound from his forehead. With proper application you can find flow in endeavors outside of creative work and athletics. A credit manager might experience flow in developing a credit-profile checklist that will do a better job of predicting the credit-worthiness of customers. A production supervisor might experience flow while conducting a performance appraisal that helps a group member to grow and develop.

The feedback you receive from doing a task correctly serves as a signal that things are going well. As the golfer hits the ball squarely in the middle of the driver, there is an immediate sound (a delightful thud) indicating that performance is on target. In addition, a pleasant vibration moves up the arm. As the truck driver maneuvers properly around a curve, he or she receives a road-hugging feeling up through the wheels, indicating that the turn has been neatly executed. As you make a presentation to higher management, and all eyes and ears are focused on you, you know you are performing well.

Despite the importance of control and feedback, the person who is experiencing flow doesn't stop to think about what is happening. It is as if you are an onlooker and the precise actions are taking place automatically. Your body is performing pleasing actions without much conscious control on your part. When you are totally absorbed in reading a book, you do not realize you are turning the pages—your fingers take over from your brain.

Considering how important flow is, it is fortunate that guidelines have been formulated to help you achieve flow in most activities. The essential steps in the process are as follows[3]:

1. Set an overall goal and as many subgoals as are realistically feasible.
2. Find ways of measuring progress in terms of the goals chosen.
3. Keep concentrating on what you are doing, and keep making finer and finer distinctions among the individual challenges involved in the activity.
4. Develop the skills necessary to capitalize on the opportunities available.
5. Keep increasing your investment of psychic energy if the activity becomes boring.

To illustrate how to achieve flow, I will use an example of an activity that bridges work and personal life: learning to read, write, and speak another language. (The same activity will enhance your magnetism.)

First, you set goals (and subgoals) and timetables for achieving them. These might include a date for mastering a beginner book or tape cassette, a date for being able to greet others in your new language, a date for being able to write postcards in your target language, and activity goals such as a certain number of hours per week devoted to watching programs in your second language on television.

Second, you will need to measure progress in terms of your goals. Attempt to read comic strips, food labels, or newspaper headlines in your target language. Measure how well you can answer questions in your language primer.

Third, concentrate. Learning a second language requires extraordinary concentration, especially if you are older than age ten. Concentrate on the sounds made by people speaking the language correctly. Look carefully at the shape of their mouths and their lip movements. If you start to daydream while studying your new language, say to yourself, "Stop. Get back on target." Trying to meet the challenges posed by learning something hard, including understanding the many nuances of your target language, should force you to concentrate.

Seek out rather than avoid the challenges of understanding in greater depth the complexity of the grammar and how to conjugate verbs. Recognize that there are no practical limits to how much there is to know about another language. Yet also recognize that you are pursuing only a certain level of mastery.

Fourth, determine what skills you do not already possess that you need for learning your language. Just the fact that you have proceeded so far would indicate the presence of several skills. Yet you may find that additional skills are necessary. For example, you may need to refresh your memorization skills. You cannot learn a second language unless you keep hundreds of words, phrases, and verb forms in your head.

Fifth, put more of yourself into the quest for learning the second language if you feel yourself becoming too detached. For instance, attempt to find your target language word for each of your most important personal possessions. The task might take a little digging in an advanced dictionary, such as learning the words for "paperweight" or "hiking boots."

Achieving flow requires that you delay immediate gratification during your search for a long-term gain. The person in search of immediate gratification tends to give up quickly when learning a complex activity. In contrast, if you invest the time in patiently developing a high skill level, you will have the opportunity to experience flow. Rarely, however, does a beginner have enough skill in a complex activity to know the joy of flow.

Display Panache

One of the most visible ways of appearing magnetic through your work is to display panache. While performing your work, look for opportunities to project flamboyance, flair, verve, spark, intensity, and other out-of-the ordinary qualities. If panache is combined with many of the other characteristics I have described throughout this book, it can give you that extra edge that helps project magnetism.

Paul Frame, the CEO of Seitel Inc., a Houston company that sells seismic data to oil and gas companies, is an example of panache in action. Even Frame's favorite hobby, racing his Ferrari in amateur competitions, reflects panache. Frame's company is often referred to as a shark tank, much to his delight. He drives the company's sales team relentlessly, creating a war room atmosphere in his sales strategy meetings. Scheduled for 7 A.M., these meetings are held virtually every workday.

During the meetings, Frame acts like a military commander marshaling his forces. Although not a native Texan, Frame has added a drawl to help establish rapport with his workers and customers. When he doesn't get an answer to a tough question, Frame puts on a grim facial expression and whistles through his teeth. He freely expresses a mean-spirited anger. On one occasion when he didn't receive an immediate answer to his question, he blurted: "Why do I have to search, like a squirrel for a nut, for this information? For me to have to dig it out, this is __________. What else is different? Tell me. Don't make me dig."

Frame says that the reason people refer to him as running a shark tank is because he tells the truth. In a shark tank, the people who fail to keep swimming perish. Frame explains how he transforms each sales representative he hires into a tough predator. "I hire smart. I manage well. I train and grow new people."[4]

Frame's uniqueness does not stem from being a tough, no-excuses manager. What differentiates him is the flare with which he exercises his toughness. Much of his panache is reflected in the way he launches the team off to battle each day and the way he combats people who fail to give him the information he needs.

Paul Frame's approach to displaying panache may not suit your style or circumstances. If you want to develop a work approach with panache, you can pick and choose among the alternatives described next:

- *Arrive at a meeting with the "wet look" in your hair, suggesting that you have just exercised and are poised to take on mighty challenges.*
- *When at a meeting, entering or exiting the building, or in the company parking lot, carry an expensive, personally purchased laptop computer.* Others seeing you will marvel at your commitment to work and information technology. You will also obtain some of the same effect by sporting a personal digital assistant. The problem, however, is that these small devices might be mistaken for a mundane pager.
- *When presenting at a meeting, use computerized presentation graphics with facility and comfort.* Don't apologize for your graphics not being as good as you would like them to be.
- *When referring to information on the screen, use a collapsible metal pointer, much like that of an army general.* Although metal pointers have been around a long time, they still add an element of flair and drama. Similarly, a laser pen that projects a small colored dot can have a dramatic effect.
- *Memorize your Internet address, and tell it to others during a work conversation.* Many people know their Internet address by heart, yet knowing yours is still an impressive touch.
- *Keep your desk and work area spotless and devoid of clutter.* If your desk is wooden, keep it so highly polished that your reflection shows. Never have more than one piece of paper on your desk when others are present. All pencils in your pencil holder should be finely sharpened and turned upward. Keep office-issue ball pens out of sight. (If you are wondering what you should do with the papers you are working on while attempting to maintain a spotless desk, use a drawer for that purpose. In this age of information technology, the smaller the amount of paper you handle, the more impressive you look.)

• *Look fresh and energetic whenever possible.* The ideal solution is to take a nap and shower just before a key meeting with insiders or customers. Fresh makeup or splashing water on your face is a compromise solution. Looking as fresh and enthusiastic at 5:30 P.M. as at 8:30 A.M. contributes to panache.

• *When talking about your work progress, make reference to a time and activity chart.* Such a chart simply maps progress on a project in terms of time checkpoints. To inject a touch of panache, a person might say, "Today is May 25. We promised to have all the negatives for the sales promotion brochures to the printer by May 31. The negatives were at the printer's this morning." Few people will question why May 31 was chosen as the checkpoint for getting material off to the printer, so you will appear very much in control and organized. And being tightly in control adds an element of panache.

• *During a meeting, mention individuals' names and make reference in rich detail to projects they are working on.* The panache will again stem from being so knowledgeable and in control about what is happening within the group.

• *Show up at a meeting in unusually casual clothes during a day not designated as a "dress down" day.* After you have provided your input, get up from your chair and say, "I would like to stay longer, folks, but my family would be upset. I'm on vacation today." Your devotion to duty will create an element of panache. Others will also admire how you do your best to balance work and family demands.

Stay Cool During a Crisis

One of the most potent forms of panache is to appear calm and in control during a crisis. Act calm yourself and make reassuring statements that will reduce the anxieties of others. Helping others through a crisis contributes directly to magnetism because people in turmoil are drawn toward a stabilizing force. Staying cool under crisis requires much more than creating an appearance of calmness. You must also engage in actions that place the crisis, or any other upsetting circumstance, under control.

James Barksdale, the magnetic and charismatic CEO of Netscape, is a world-class example of coolness under crisis. In his days at Federal Express, he worked his way through the tough times of doing battle against the giant UPS (then known as United Parcel Service). Later he became a key figure at McCaw Communication when the company fought valiantly against AT&T.

In the mid-1990s he was instrumental in navigating Netscape through the near-crisis caused by Microsoft Corp. Bill Gates and Microsoft decided to challenge Netscape Navigator's dominance in providing Internet devices. Even during the times when the competitive threat was most intense, Barksdale had a calming and reassuring effect on his employees. He helped them believe that the company's product line would not be snuffed out by Microsoft. He calmly and confidently reassured workers that Netscape had a wonderful product that was needed by millions of computer users.

You do not have to rely on intuition alone to manage a crisis or near-crisis. If you follow certain logical steps you improve your chances for overcoming the crisis and enhancing your magnetism in the process. The six steps are as follows:

1. *Calm down and start thinking.* No matter how bad the crisis is, take at least an hour or two to think before acting. Impulsive acts might dig you—and the company—into a bigger hole.
2. *Clarify the problem.* What is the real problem created by this crisis? Perhaps the crisis has created a credibility problem or a financial problem. Sometimes the crisis has created both, such as a defective product that threatens the health of consumers.
3. *Search for creative alternatives.* What options are open? Many managers facing a crisis choose stonewalling over dealing with the problem openly. In the process they exacerbate the crisis.
4. *Make a choice.* If the crisis is to be resolved, you must make a tough decision at some point.
5. *Develop an action plan and implement it.* Now that you have chosen an alternative solution, formulate the specific steps that must be taken to get out of the mess.
6. *Evaluate outcomes.* Did the crisis-management plan work or will you have to try another alternative? A cautionary note: If your first plan fails, you may not be invited to try another.

Stan Carson worked as a service engineer for a manufacturer of computer-based medical equipment. His personal experience, given in his own words, provides an apt example of crisis management:

> I volunteered for a suicide mission and came back alive. The project required the development of a game plan for the national installation of a major software upgrade. This was a critical project because the upgrade was supposed to solve several serious problems plaguing the equipment. We had lost key accounts, and the other users were screaming. If all the accounts had left, the company would have faced bankruptcy.
>
> Another gory detail was that the upgrade had to be accomplished with the minimum amount of machine downtime. I would be personally responsible for contacting each district service manager and coordinating with him or her the schedule of service technician training, shipment of the upgrade kit, and the installation schedule. Any problems that occurred would be directly attributed to me. Such was the suicide portion of the project.
>
> Just when I was about to implement the first upgrade, my manager wanted to see me right away. He told me that the director of marketing and service and the national service manager wanted a presentation of my game plan. Fortunately, I had enough sense to have quickly but carefully developed one.
>
> The emergency upgrades solved the software problems. Several district service managers called my manager to express gratitude for my support. Volunteering for a project whose failure could have meant my demise worked for me. Everybody in the executive suite knew who I was, and I had also created other allies in the company.

Stan successfully managed a crisis and thereby elevated his status in the company. Having successfully managed a crisis also added an element of magnetism to Stan's personality that would enhance his chances for promotion to a management job. Furthermore, Stan received excellent experience. Crises are inevitable in business organizations, and crisis managers will always be in demand.

Stan followed the precepts of crisis management in that he had a game plan based on a careful assessment of available alternatives.

Like other successful crisis managers, Stan is now known as a troubleshooter—a reputation that contributes strongly to magnetism.

Be Multifaceted

A long-term approach to enhancing your magnetism through work is to be multidimensional and multifaceted. Impress and astonish others with the fact that you have depth in several domains. For example, the MBA graduates most in demand are those who also possess knowledge about information technology or manufacturing technology. Having both business knowledge and technology knowledge makes for a powerful combination. Even more in demand for high-level assignments are those MBAs with a third marketable facet—fluency in a second language.

One way of being multifaceted is to have enough knowledge and skill to earn a living in more than one domain. An example would be a marketing specialist who could also be credible as a production supervisor. A multifaceted person is sometimes referred to as a cluster specialist, or a person who has technical depth in related technologies, crafts, markets, or skills.

> Elvin Montogmery, a clinical psychologist and consultant with Arthur Young, is an example of a cluster specialist. He notes: "I didn't want to be limited by traditional psychology. But I didn't want to abandon all I had learned." Following an intense interest in what makes an effective clinic, he wrote his dissertation on the clinic rather than on the patient. "Eventually I saw myself as a therapist of organizations rather than individuals."
>
> By both generalizing and integrating his skills, knowledge, and interests, Montgomery created a cluster specialty: social systems, organizational behavior, and new organizations. This was exactly the constellation of skills and interests Arthur Young needed to adapt a Swedish intrapreneurial (entrepreneurs within a large corporation) program to American business. The same cluster of skills was also needed to manage the new Arthur Young intrapreneurial program.[5] Having this unusual skill cluster added to Montgomery's magnetism.

Many people are unable or unwilling to make the commitment to becoming a credible specialist in more than one field. If this is your situation, you can capitalize on the importance of being multifaceted in another way. Becoming a cross-functional (or multidisciplinary) thinker will add to your magnetism in the modern organization.

The cross-functional thinker thinks across the functions for the good of the total organization. He or she thinks like a general manager or CEO, showing no favoritism toward a specific business function. In the process, the cross-functional thinker looks at problems from a broad, or multidisciplinary, perspective. Visualize the following scenario:

You are asked to investigate customer complaints that your product is too expensive. Functional viewpoints on the problem are as follows:

- Finance must find a way to lower the cost. Costs are obviously out of line.
- Manufacturing must squeeze some more cost out of the product. (Maybe it can buy lower-priced components and cut down on overtime.)
- Marketing must find a way to explain why this product is a bargain at its current price.
- Engineering must incorporate a new high-tech feature that will dazzle customers and make them forget about price.

A person with cross-functional thinking will look at several perspectives in solving the problem and encourage co-workers to do the same. From the cross-functional perspective, the team has a *business* problem—not a finance, marketing, manufacturing, or engineering problem.

The team player with effective cross-functional skills understands the perspectives of the various disciplines. He or she uses empathy to find common interests and build bridges across disciplines. A finance specialist assigned to a quality improvement team made this comment with respect to resolving a customer complaint about price: "I don't care whose ox gets gored. Let's satisfy the customer and make some money at the same time."

Developing a cross-functional perspective can be approached in several ways, all centering around the idea of shedding the functional viewpoint. Three additional suggestions follow:

1. *Keep in mind the venerable analogy about wearing different hats.* Think about owning a functional hat and a cross-functional hat. Choose which hat to wear on a given day. Should you be assigned to a cross-functional team, wear your cross-functional hat.

2. *Imagine that you are a general manager.* You can stimulate your cross-functional thinking by imagining yourself as a general manager facing the problem at hand.

3. *Take advantage of any opportunity for multidisciplinary training.* An elegant way to develop cross-functional skills and thinking is to participate in multifunctional development. Such development is usually reserved for managers, but professional and technical workers sometimes participate. Multifunctional development is an intentional effort to enhance the capacity of selected individuals by exposing them to various functions within an organization.

Any opportunity along these lines that you can grab will help you think cross-functionally. Furthermore, it will help groom you for promotion and make at least a small contribution to your magnetism. A fundamental truth about vertical mobility is that broad experience enhances promotability.

The following exercise in cross-functional thinking will show you how one scenario might go.

How to Be a Cross-Functional Thinker

Pretend you are a member of a process redesign team. The team is about to recommend eliminating outside sales representatives for a particular product line. From a self-interested point of view, the marketing representative would ordinarily think, "There goes the outside sales group right out the door." The human resources representative might say, "There goes my program for recruiting, selecting, and training outside sales representatives."

To prevent self-interested, functional thinking from snowballing, you say, "Let's look at our redesign plan as if we were all general managers. What redesign solutions will benefit the organization as a whole? For now, let's forget about which functional group will take the biggest hit. What counts is the long-term health of the entire organization." (Bravo, magnetism.)

Be a Fixit Person

As previously mentioned, being a troubleshooter adds to your magnetism. And it is equally true that a person who develops the reputation for being able to fix difficult problems will be perceived as magnetic. Don't you find someone who can rescue you from your problems appealing? In the current era, workers everywhere are drawn to the information technology expert who can help them untangle their computer problems. The computer fixit person who provides this type of assistance, especially when it is not his or her official job, gains extra stature.

> Developing a reputation as a fixit person can also take place at the managerial level. Roger A. Enrico, the CEO of PepsiCo, represents an excellent corporate example. Dating back to the early 1960s, Enrico played a major role in turning around each of the soft drink and snack food giant's three businesses. To add to his magnetism, Enrico was the creative mastermind behind the resurgence of Pizza Hut Inc. in the mid-1990s.
>
> The winning strategy for boosting Pizza Hut sales was formulated when Enrico noticed a promising new product in development. It was a pizza with a ring of mozzarella baked into the outer edges of the crust. He decided to prime the product as part of a $100 million advertising campaign. Within its first year, Stuffed Crust Pizza racked up revenues of $1 billion.[6] Even though Enrico did not invent the pizza with stuffed crust, he had the good sense to gamble on it as a breakthrough product.

How much magnetism one gains from fixing problems depends on certain characteristics of the problem and the situation. A fixit person is likely to be perceived as more magnetic when:

- The problem is important to the organization, such as getting software configurations to run or revitalizing a major product.
- Others talk about the problem you fixed, or you subtly let others know about your good deeds.
- You fix the problems with a positive attitude rather than bemoaning the fact that you get stuck with the worst assignments.

- You thank others for having given you the opportunity to be of help.

Welcome Change

Yet another way of becoming more personally magnetic is to welcome change in your work environment. People who welcome constructive change rather than fighting it set a good example for others. If you are the person who shows others how change, such as a reorganization or a new benefits package, can be beneficial, others will be drawn to you. By welcoming the inevitable, you are a pathfinder who gives others the structure and guidance they need.

Many people are fearful of change because they think it will be disadvantageous in one way or another. Also, they may not want to experience the discomfort of changing comfortable habits. By welcoming change, you demonstrate a willingness to take risks and experience the unknown. Others will be drawn to you because you show the spirit of adventure, inquiry, and flexibility that is characteristic of the personally magnetic.

In this final chapter we have explored how you can display personal magnetism through your work. Your performance and attitudes toward work can be a force for demonstrating your magnetic qualities. In quick review, consider these strategies:

1. Strive for peak performance.
2. Display panache in your work approach.
3. Stay cool during a crisis.
4. Be multifaceted (such as having a cluster of valuable skills).
5. Be a fixit person.
6. Welcome change.

Thank you for sharing my belief that people can enhance their magnetism and charisma by implementing the right strategies and tactics. Best of luck in enhancing your personal magnetism.

Appendix: Witty Responses for Chapter 8

Many different responses are possible to the scenarios in question. Also, when making your comments, your extraverbal communication can contribute mightily to your verbal comments. Making a witty comment involves both good timing and the right verbal expression.

Scenario 1: "I have some good news and bad news today. The good news is that we are going to be talking about increasing productivity. Top management is so interested in improving productivity, it is beginning by withholding salary adjustments for this year. By reducing costs, productivity will be increased."

Scenario 2: "I'm sorry to hear that your son is temporarily lost in cyberspace. But with his expertise on the Net, I'm sure he can get a job. Perhaps he'll appreciate college more after he returns from cyberspace."

Scenario 3: "I guess our vice president made two errors. First she believed too much in sisterhood. Second, she didn't keep enough secrets to make herself indispensable. I bet she'll be much wiser in her next job. Or maybe she can become her old assistant's assistant!"

Notes

Chapter 1

1. "A Mellower Mickey Kantor?" *Business Week*, June 17, 1996, pp. 138–142.
2. Adapted from Bernard Keys and Thomas Case, "How to Become an Influential Manager," *Academy of Management Executive*, November 1990, pp. 45–46.
3. Patricia Sellers, "Women, Sex & Power," *Fortune*, August 5, 1996, p. 47.
4. Based partially on "Self-Esteem and Peak Performance: How to Improve Your Attitude, Productivity, and Satisfaction on the Job," *Career Track* brochure and seminar, 1994.
5. Robert McGarvey, "Mind Power," *Entrepreneur*, May 1995, p. 103.
6. Gail Edmonson, "A Blueprint from Europe," *Business Week*, February 5, 1996, p. 42.

Chapter 2

1. "Scott McNealy's Rising Sun: How He's Taking the Computer Maker to New Heights," *Business Week*, January 22, 1996, p. 66.
2. Robert D. Hof, "The Education of Andrew Grove," *Business Week*, January 16, 1995, pp. 60–62.
3. Chris Argyris, "Teaching Smart People How to Learn," *Harvard Business Review*, May–June 1991, pp. 99–109.
4. Robert S. Wieder, "How to Get Great Ideas," *Success*, November 1983, p. 30.
5. Eugene Raudsepp, "Exercises for Creative Growth, *Success*, February 1981, pp. 46–47; and Andrew J. DuBrin, *Reengineering Survival Guide* (Cincinnati, Ohio: Thomson Executive Press, 1996), pp. 57–69.
6. Based on facts reported in Nancy K. Austin, "Managing by Parable," *Working Woman*, September 1995, pp. 15–16.
7. Jay T. Knippen and Thad B. Green, "Building Self-Confidence," *Supervisory Management*, August 1989, pp. 22–27.

Chapter 3

1. Quoted in James M. Kouzes and Barry Z. Posner, *The Leadership Challenge: How to Get Extraordinary Things Done in Organizations* (San Francisco: Jossey-Bass, 1987), p. 270.

2. Debra Phillips, "The Joy of Business: Keeping the Passion Alive in Your Company," *Entrepreneur*, August 1995, p. 144.
3. Shawn Tully, "So, Mr. Bossidy, We Know You Can Cut. Now Show Us How to Grow," *Fortune*, August 21, 1995, pp. 72–73.
4. Jeffrey Pfeffer, *Managing with Power: Politics and Influence in Organizations* (Boston, Mass.: Harvard Business School Press, 1992), p. 224.
5. Anat Rafeli and Robert I. Sutton, "Expression of Emotion as Part of the Work Role," *Academy of Management Review*, January 1987, p. 31.
6. Linda Grant, "Stirring It Up at Campbell," *Fortune*, May 13, 1996, p. 80.

Chapter 4

1. Suggestions 1 through 5 are based on "Body Language," *Executive Strategies*, June 5, 1990, p. 8.
2. Patricia Sellers, "Women, Sex & Power," *Fortune*, August 5, 1996, p. 46.
3. Kathleen Driscoll, "Your Voice Can Make or Break You," *Rochester (N.Y.) Democrat and Chronicle*, August 26, 1993, p. 10B.
4. William Nabers, "The New Corporate Uniforms," *Fortune*, November 13, 1995, p. 135.

Chapter 5

1. Research reported in Laura Lippman, "The Age of Obsequiousness: Flattering Your Way Up the Corporate Ladder," *Baltimore Sun*, October 24, 1994, p. 1D
2. Ibid., p. 2D.
3. "Flattery Works," *Executive Strategies*, September 4, 1990, p. 4.

Chapter 6

1. Andrew Kupfer, "Craig Sees an Internet in the Sky," *Fortune*, May 27, 1996, p. 64.
2. Kenneth Labich, "First: 65 Candles, A Two-Mile Run, & a 10,000-Foot Plunge," *Fortune*, July 22, 1996, pp. 21–22.
3. Robert McGarvey, "Soul Man," *Entrepreneur*, October 1995, pp. 144–149; additional data on book sales collected in September 1996.
4. Michael Oneal, "God, Family, and Domino's—That's It," *Business Week*, January 30, 1995, p. 57.
5. Peter Burrows, "Micron's Comeback Kid," *Business Week*, May 13, 1996, p. 74.
6. "The Shredder: Did CEO Dunlap Save Scott Paper—Or Just Pretty It Up?" *Business Week*, January 15, 1996, pp. 56–61.
7. Marlene Caroselli, *The Language of Leadership* (Amherst, Mass.: Human Resource Development Press, 1990), p. 11.

Chapter 7

1. Jeffrey Keller, "Associate with Positive People," *A Supplement to the Pryor Report*) (Clemson, S.C.: *The Pryor Report*, 1994), pp. 1–4.

2. Gerald Graham, "Management Issues," *Rochester (N.Y.) Democrat and Chronicle*, August 26, 1996, p. 5D.
3. Justin Martin, "Tomorrow's CEOs," *Fortune*, June 26, 1996, pp. 77–78.
4. Ibid., p. 88.
5. Roger Dawson, *Secrets of Power Persuasion: Everything You'll Ever Need to Get Anything You'll Ever Want* (Englewood Cliffs, N.J.: Prentice Hall, 1992), pp. 181–183.
6. The first three suggestions are from Connirae Andreas and Steve Andreas, *Heart of the Mind* (Moab, Utah: Real People Press, 1991).

Chapter 8

1. Robert Orben, "Why Humor?" *Current Comedy* (Wilmington, Del., Newsletter), 1987, p. 1.
2. Updated from John Cleese, "Serious Talk About Humor in the Office," *Wall Street Journal*, August 1, 1988.
3. Bruce Avolio and Jane Howell, "A Funny Thing Happened on the Way to the Bottom Line," paper presented at the Society of Industrial and Organizational Psychology, San Diego, California, August 9, 1996.
4. W. Jack Duncan and J. Philip Feisal, "No Laughing Matter: Patterns of Humor in the Workplace," *Organizational Dynamics*, Spring 1989, pp. 18–19.
5. Wilma Davidson, "Add Humor to Workplace Memos," *Personnel Journal*, June 1992, p. 67.
6. Shari Caudron, "Humor Is Healthy in the Workplace," *Personnel Journal*, June 1992, p. 63.
7. Karen Karvonen, "Funny Business," *USAIR*, October 1988, p. 38.
8. Jokes 2, 3, 4, and 5 are from Vince Spezzano, "Why Do People Laugh at Jokes?" *Rochester (N.Y.) Democrat and Chronicle*, April 22, 1990, pp. 1D, 2D.
9. Karvonen, "Funny Business," p. 37.
10. Duncan and Feisal, "No Laughing Matter," p. 18.
11. The ideas for the suggestions presented here come from various sources, including "Why Leaders Laugh," *Executive Strategies*, November 1995, pp. 3–4; Larry Wilde, "Beat Stress: Stress Humor," *Association Management*, July 1988, p. 130; and Lindsay Collier, "The Effect of Humor on the Work Environment," unpublished paper distributed within Eastman Kodak, Rochester, N.Y., July 25, 1989.

Chapter 9

1. The books on neurolinguistic programming most relied on here are Sue Knight, *NLP at Work: The Difference that Makes a Difference in Business* (London: Nicholas Brealey, 1995) and Joseph O'Connor and John Seymour, *Introducing Neuro-Linguistic Programming: Psychological Skills for Understanding and Influencing People* (London: The Acquarian Press, 1990).
2. "Sales Arsenal," *Success*, May 1966, p. 74.
3. Adapted from *NLP at Work: The Difference that Makes a Difference in Business*

by Sue Knight, 1995. Published by Nicholas Brealey Publishing, 36 John Street, London WC1N 2AT, UK. Fax = 44 (0) 171 404 8311.

4. O'Connor and Seymour, *Introducing Neuro-Linguistic Programming,* p. 20.

Chapter 10

1. Charles Garfield, *Peak Performers: The New Heroes of American Business* (New York: Avon Books, 1987), pp. 22–52; Ingrid Lorch-Bacci, "Achieving Peak Performance," *Executive Management Forum,* January 1991, pp. 1–4; and Michael Rozek, "Can You Spot a Peak Performer?" *Personnel Journal,* June 1991, pp. 77–78.
2. Garfield, *Peak Performers,* p. 40.
3. Mihaly Csikszentmihalyi, *Flow: The Psychology of Optimal Experience* (New York: Harper Perennial, 1990), p. 97.
4. Michael Warshaw, "Shark Tank Selling," *Success,* May 1995, pp. 52–54.
5. Beverly A. Potter, "Intrapreneurs: New Corporate Breed," *Business Week's Guide to Careers,* December 1985, p. 66.
6. Lori Bongiorno, "The Pepsi Generation," *Business Week,* March 11, 1996, pp. 70–73.

Index